Mometrix
TEST PREPARATION

Virginia SOL Grade 3 Secrets Study Guide

Dear Future Exam Success Story

First of all, **THANK YOU** for purchasing Mometrix study materials!

Second, congratulations! You are one of the few determined test-takers who are committed to doing whatever it takes to excel on your exam. **You have come to the right place.** We developed these study materials with one goal in mind: to deliver you the information you need in a format that's concise and easy to use.

In addition to optimizing your guide for the content of the test, we've outlined our recommended steps for breaking down the preparation process into small, attainable goals so you can make sure you stay on track.

We've also analyzed the entire test-taking process, identifying the most common pitfalls and showing how you can overcome them and be ready for any curveball the test throws you.

Standardized testing is one of the biggest obstacles on your road to success, which only increases the importance of doing well in the high-pressure, high-stakes environment of test day. Your results on this test could have a significant impact on your future, and this guide provides the information and practical advice to help you achieve your full potential on test day.

Your success is our success

We would love to hear from you! If you would like to share the story of your exam success or if you have any questions or comments in regard to our products, please contact us at **800-673-8175** or **support@mometrix.com**.

Thanks again for your business and we wish you continued success!

Sincerely,
The Mometrix Test Preparation Team

Need more help? Check out our flashcards at:
http://MometrixFlashcards.com/SOL

Written and edited by the Mometrix Exam Secrets Test Prep Team
Printed in the United States of America

TABLE OF CONTENTS

Introduction

Thank you for purchasing this resource! You have made the choice to prepare yourself for a test that could have a huge impact on your future, and this guide is designed to help you be fully ready for test day. Obviously, it's important to have a solid understanding of the test material, but you also need to be prepared for the unique environment and stressors of the test, so that you can perform to the best of your abilities.

For this purpose, the first section that appears in this guide is the **Secret Keys**. We've devoted countless hours to meticulously researching what works and what doesn't, and we've boiled down our findings to the five most impactful steps you can take to improve your performance on the test. We start at the beginning with study planning and move through the preparation process, all the way to the testing strategies that will help you get the most out of what you know when you're finally sitting in front of the test.

We recommend that you start preparing for your test as far in advance as possible. However, if you've bought this guide as a last-minute study resource and only have a few days before your test, we recommend that you skip over the first two Secret Keys since they address a long-term study plan.

If you struggle with **test anxiety**, we strongly encourage you to check out our recommendations for how you can overcome it. Test anxiety is a formidable foe, but it can be beaten, and we want to make sure you have the tools you need to defeat it.

Secret Key #1 – Plan Big, Study Small

There's a lot riding on your performance. If you want to ace this test, you're going to need to keep your skills sharp and the material fresh in your mind. You need a plan that lets you review everything you need to know while still fitting in your schedule. We'll break this strategy down into three categories.

Information Organization

Start with the information you already have: the official test outline. From this, you can make a complete list of all the concepts you need to cover before the test. Organize these concepts into groups that can be studied together, and create a list of any related vocabulary you need to learn so you can brush up on any difficult terms. You'll want to keep this vocabulary list handy once you actually start studying since you may need to add to it along the way.

Time Management

Once you have your set of study concepts, decide how to spread them out over the time you have left before the test. Break your study plan into small, clear goals so you have a manageable task for each day and know exactly what you're doing. Then just focus on one small step at a time. When you manage your time this way, you don't need to spend hours at a time studying. Studying a small block of content for a short period each day helps you retain information better and avoid stressing over how much you have left to do. You can relax knowing that you have a plan to cover everything in time. In order for this strategy to be effective though, you have to start studying early and stick to your schedule. Avoid the exhaustion and futility that comes from last-minute cramming!

Study Environment

The environment you study in has a big impact on your learning. Studying in a coffee shop, while probably more enjoyable, is not likely to be as fruitful as studying in a quiet room. It's important to keep distractions to a minimum. You're only planning to study for a short block of time, so make the most of it. Don't pause to check your phone or get up to find a snack. It's also important to **avoid multitasking**. Research has consistently shown that multitasking will make your studying dramatically less effective. Your study area should also be comfortable and well-lit so you don't have the distraction of straining your eyes or sitting on an uncomfortable chair.

The time of day you study is also important. You want to be rested and alert. Don't wait until just before bedtime. Study when you'll be most likely to comprehend and remember. Even better, if you know what time of day your test will be, set that time aside for study. That way your brain will be used to working on that subject at that specific time and you'll have a better chance of recalling information.

Finally, it can be helpful to team up with others who are studying for the same test. Your actual studying should be done in as isolated an environment as possible, but the work of organizing the information and setting up the study plan can be divided up. In between study sessions, you can discuss with your teammates the concepts that you're all studying and quiz each other on the details. Just be sure that your teammates are as serious about the test as you are. If you find that your study time is being replaced with social time, you might need to find a new team.

Secret Key #2 – Make Your Studying Count

You're devoting a lot of time and effort to preparing for this test, so you want to be absolutely certain it will pay off. This means doing more than just reading the content and hoping you can remember it on test day. It's important to make every minute of study count. There are two main areas you can focus on to make your studying count.

Retention

It doesn't matter how much time you study if you can't remember the material. You need to make sure you are retaining the concepts. To check your retention of the information you're learning, try recalling it at later times with minimal prompting. Try carrying around flashcards and glance at one or two from time to time or ask a friend who's also studying for the test to quiz you.

To enhance your retention, look for ways to put the information into practice so that you can apply it rather than simply recalling it. If you're using the information in practical ways, it will be much easier to remember. Similarly, it helps to solidify a concept in your mind if you're not only reading it to yourself but also explaining it to someone else. Ask a friend to let you teach them about a concept you're a little shaky on (or speak aloud to an imaginary audience if necessary). As you try to summarize, define, give examples, and answer your friend's questions, you'll understand the concepts better and they will stay with you longer. Finally, step back for a big picture view and ask yourself how each piece of information fits with the whole subject. When you link the different concepts together and see them working together as a whole, it's easier to remember the individual components.

Finally, practice showing your work on any multi-step problems, even if you're just studying. Writing out each step you take to solve a problem will help solidify the process in your mind, and you'll be more likely to remember it during the test.

Modality

Modality simply refers to the means or method by which you study. Choosing a study modality that fits your own individual learning style is crucial. No two people learn best in exactly the same way, so it's important to know your strengths and use them to your advantage.

For example, if you learn best by visualization, focus on visualizing a concept in your mind and draw an image or a diagram. Try color-coding your notes, illustrating them, or creating symbols that will trigger your mind to recall a learned concept. If you learn best by hearing or discussing information, find a study partner who learns the same way or read aloud to yourself. Think about how to put the information in your own words. Imagine that you are giving a lecture on the topic and record yourself so you can listen to it later.

For any learning style, flashcards can be helpful. Organize the information so you can take advantage of spare moments to review. Underline key words or phrases. Use different colors for different categories. Mnemonic devices (such as creating a short list in which every item starts with the same letter) can also help with retention. Find what works best for you and use it to store the information in your mind most effectively and easily.

Secret Key #3 – Practice the Right Way

Your success on test day depends not only on how many hours you put into preparing, but also on whether you prepared the right way. It's good to check along the way to see if your studying is paying off. One of the most effective ways to do this is by taking practice tests to evaluate your progress. Practice tests are useful because they show exactly where you need to improve. Every time you take a practice test, pay special attention to these three groups of questions:

- The questions you got wrong
- The questions you had to guess on, even if you guessed right
- The questions you found difficult or slow to work through

This will show you exactly what your weak areas are, and where you need to devote more study time. Ask yourself why each of these questions gave you trouble. Was it because you didn't understand the material? Was it because you didn't remember the vocabulary? Do you need more repetitions on this type of question to build speed and confidence? Dig into those questions and figure out how you can strengthen your weak areas as you go back to review the material.

Additionally, many practice tests have a section explaining the answer choices. It can be tempting to read the explanation and think that you now have a good understanding of the concept. However, an explanation likely only covers part of the question's broader context. Even if the explanation makes perfect sense, **go back and investigate** every concept related to the question until you're positive you have a thorough understanding.

As you go along, keep in mind that the practice test is just that: practice. Memorizing these questions and answers will not be very helpful on the actual test because it is unlikely to have any of the same exact questions. If you only know the right answers to the sample questions, you won't be prepared for the real thing. **Study the concepts** until you understand them fully, and then you'll be able to answer any question that shows up on the test.

It's important to wait on the practice tests until you're ready. If you take a test on your first day of study, you may be overwhelmed by the amount of material covered and how much you need to learn. Work up to it gradually.

On test day, you'll need to be prepared for answering questions, managing your time, and using the test-taking strategies you've learned. It's a lot to balance, like a mental marathon that will have a big impact on your future. Like training for a marathon, you'll need to start slowly and work your way up. When test day arrives, you'll be ready.

Start with the strategies you've read in the first two Secret Keys—plan your course and study in the way that works best for you. If you have time, consider using multiple study resources to get different approaches to the same concepts. It can be helpful to see difficult concepts from more than one angle. Then find a good source for practice tests. Many times, the test website will suggest potential study resources or provide sample tests.

Practice Test Strategy

If you're able to find at least three practice tests, we recommend this strategy:

Untimed and Open-Book Practice

Take the first test with no time constraints and with your notes and study guide handy. Take your time and focus on applying the strategies you've learned.

Timed and Open-Book Practice

Take the second practice test open-book as well, but set a timer and practice pacing yourself to finish in time.

Timed and Closed-Book Practice

Take any other practice tests as if it were test day. Set a timer and put away your study materials. Sit at a table or desk in a quiet room, imagine yourself at the testing center, and answer questions as quickly and accurately as possible.

Keep repeating timed and closed-book tests on a regular basis until you run out of practice tests or it's time for the actual test. Your mind will be ready for the schedule and stress of test day, and you'll be able to focus on recalling the material you've learned.

Secret Key #4 – Pace Yourself

Once you're fully prepared for the material on the test, your biggest challenge on test day will be managing your time. Just knowing that the clock is ticking can make you panic even if you have plenty of time left. Work on pacing yourself so you can build confidence against the time constraints of the exam. Pacing is a difficult skill to master, especially in a high-pressure environment, so **practice is vital**.

Set time expectations for your pace based on how much time is available. For example, if a section has 60 questions and the time limit is 30 minutes, you know you have to average 30 seconds or less per question in order to answer them all. Although 30 seconds is the hard limit, set 25 seconds per question as your goal, so you reserve extra time to spend on harder questions. When you budget extra time for the harder questions, you no longer have any reason to stress when those questions take longer to answer.

Don't let this time expectation distract you from working through the test at a calm, steady pace, but keep it in mind so you don't spend too much time on any one question. Recognize that taking extra time on one question you don't understand may keep you from answering two that you do understand later in the test. If your time limit for a question is up and you're still not sure of the answer, mark it and move on, and come back to it later if the time and the test format allow. If the testing format doesn't allow you to return to earlier questions, just make an educated guess; then put it out of your mind and move on.

On the easier questions, be careful not to rush. It may seem wise to hurry through them so you have more time for the challenging ones, but it's not worth missing one if you know the concept and just didn't take the time to read the question fully. Work efficiently but make sure you understand the question and have looked at all of the answer choices, since more than one may seem right at first.

Even if you're paying attention to the time, you may find yourself a little behind at some point. You should speed up to get back on track, but do so wisely. Don't panic; just take a few seconds less on each question until you're caught up. Don't guess without thinking, but do look through the answer choices and eliminate any you know are wrong. If you can get down to two choices, it is often worthwhile to guess from those. Once you've chosen an answer, move on and don't dwell on any that you skipped or had to hurry through. If a question was taking too long, chances are it was one of the harder ones, so you weren't as likely to get it right anyway.

On the other hand, if you find yourself getting ahead of schedule, it may be beneficial to slow down a little. The more quickly you work, the more likely you are to make a careless mistake that will affect your score. You've budgeted time for each question, so don't be afraid to spend that time. Practice an efficient but careful pace to get the most out of the time you have.

Secret Key #5 – Have a Plan for Guessing

When you're taking the test, you may find yourself stuck on a question. Some of the answer choices seem better than others, but you don't see the one answer choice that is obviously correct. What do you do?

The scenario described above is very common, yet most test takers have not effectively prepared for it. Developing and practicing a plan for guessing may be one of the single most effective uses of your time as you get ready for the exam.

In developing your plan for guessing, there are three questions to address:

- When should you start the guessing process?
- How should you narrow down the choices?
- Which answer should you choose?

When to Start the Guessing Process

Unless your plan for guessing is to select C every time (which, despite its merits, is not what we recommend), you need to leave yourself enough time to apply your answer elimination strategies. Since you have a limited amount of time for each question, that means that if you're going to give yourself the best shot at guessing correctly, you have to decide quickly whether or not you will guess.

Of course, the best-case scenario is that you don't have to guess at all, so first, see if you can answer the question based on your knowledge of the subject and basic reasoning skills. Focus on the key words in the question and try to jog your memory of related topics. Give yourself a chance to bring the knowledge to mind, but once you realize that you don't have (or you can't access) the knowledge you need to answer the question, it's time to start the guessing process.

It's almost always better to start the guessing process too early than too late. It only takes a few seconds to remember something and answer the question from knowledge. Carefully eliminating wrong answer choices takes longer. Plus, going through the process of eliminating answer choices can actually help jog your memory.

Summary: Start the guessing process as soon as you decide that you can't answer the question based on your knowledge.

How to Narrow Down the Choices

The next chapter in this book (**Test-Taking Strategies**) includes a wide range of strategies for how to approach questions and how to look for answer choices to eliminate. You will definitely want to read those carefully, practice them, and figure out which ones work best for you. Here though, we're going to address a mindset rather than a particular strategy.

Your odds of guessing an answer correctly depend on how many options you are choosing from.

Number of options left	5	4	3	2	1
Odds of guessing correctly	20%	25%	33%	50%	100%

You can see from this chart just how valuable it is to be able to eliminate incorrect answers and make an educated guess, but there are two things that many test takers do that cause them to miss out on the benefits of guessing:

- Accidentally eliminating the correct answer
- Selecting an answer based on an impression

We'll look at the first one here, and the second one in the next section.

To avoid accidentally eliminating the correct answer, we recommend a thought exercise called **the $5 challenge**. In this challenge, you only eliminate an answer choice from contention if you are willing to bet $5 on it being wrong. Why $5? Five dollars is a small but not insignificant amount of money. It's an amount you could afford to lose but wouldn't want to throw away. And while losing $5 once might not hurt too much, doing it twenty times will set you back $100. In the same way, each small decision you make—eliminating a choice here, guessing on a question there—won't by itself impact your score very much, but when you put them all together, they can make a big difference. By holding each answer choice elimination decision to a higher standard, you can reduce the risk of accidentally eliminating the correct answer.

The $5 challenge can also be applied in a positive sense: If you are willing to bet $5 that an answer choice *is* correct, go ahead and mark it as correct.

Summary: Only eliminate an answer choice if you are willing to bet $5 that it is wrong.

Which Answer to Choose

You're taking the test. You've run into a hard question and decided you'll have to guess. You've eliminated all the answer choices you're willing to bet $5 on. Now you have to pick an answer. Why do we even need to talk about this? Why can't you just pick whichever one you feel like when the time comes?

The answer to these questions is that if you don't come into the test with a plan, you'll rely on your impression to select an answer choice, and if you do that, you risk falling into a trap. The test writers know that everyone who takes their test will be guessing on some of the questions, so they intentionally write wrong answer choices to seem plausible. You still have to pick an answer though, and if the wrong answer choices are designed to look right, how can you ever be sure that you're not falling for their trap? The best solution we've found to this dilemma is to take the decision out of your hands entirely. Here is the process we recommend:

Once you've eliminated any choices that you are confident (willing to bet $5) are wrong, select the first remaining choice as your answer.

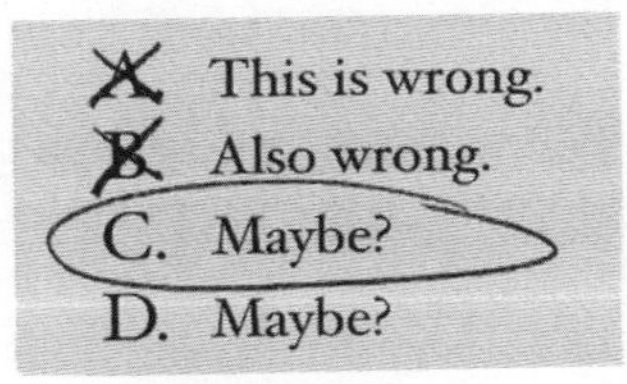

Whether you choose to select the first remaining choice, the second, or the last, the important thing is that you use some preselected standard. Using this approach guarantees that you will not be enticed into selecting an answer choice that looks right, because you are not basing your decision on how the answer choices look.

This is not meant to make you question your knowledge. Instead, it is to help you recognize the difference between your knowledge and your impressions. There's a huge difference between thinking an answer is right because of what you know, and thinking an answer is right because it looks or sounds like it should be right.

Summary: To ensure that your selection is appropriately random, make a predetermined selection from among all answer choices you have not eliminated.

Test-Taking Strategies

This section contains a list of test-taking strategies that you may find helpful as you work through the test. By taking what you know and applying logical thought, you can maximize your chances of answering any question correctly!

It is very important to realize that every question is different and every person is different: no single strategy will work on every question, and no single strategy will work for every person. That's why we've included all of them here, so you can try them out and determine which ones work best for different types of questions and which ones work best for you.

Question Strategies

☑ Read Carefully

Read the question and the answer choices carefully. Don't miss the question because you misread the terms. You have plenty of time to read each question thoroughly and make sure you understand what is being asked. Yet a happy medium must be attained, so don't waste too much time. You must read carefully and efficiently.

☑ Contextual Clues

Look for contextual clues. If the question includes a word you are not familiar with, look at the immediate context for some indication of what the word might mean. Contextual clues can often give you all the information you need to decipher the meaning of an unfamiliar word. Even if you can't determine the meaning, you may be able to narrow down the possibilities enough to make a solid guess at the answer to the question.

☑ Prefixes

If you're having trouble with a word in the question or answer choices, try dissecting it. Take advantage of every clue that the word might include. Prefixes can be a huge help. Usually, they allow you to determine a basic meaning. *Pre-* means before, *post-* means after, *pro-* is positive, *de-* is negative. From prefixes, you can get an idea of the general meaning of the word and try to put it into context.

☑ Hedge Words

Watch out for critical hedge words, such as *likely, may, can, often, almost, mostly, usually, generally, rarely,* and *sometimes.* Question writers insert these hedge phrases to cover every possibility. Often an answer choice will be wrong simply because it leaves no room for exception. Be on guard for answer choices that have definitive words such as *exactly* and *always.*

☑ Switchback Words

Stay alert for *switchbacks.* These are the words and phrases frequently used to alert you to shifts in thought. The most common switchback words are *but, although,* and *however.* Others include *nevertheless, on the other hand, even though, while, in spite of, despite,* and *regardless of.* Switchback words are important to catch because they can change the direction of the question or an answer choice.

⊘ Face Value

When in doubt, use common sense. Accept the situation in the problem at face value. Don't read too much into it. These problems will not require you to make wild assumptions. If you have to go beyond creativity and warp time or space in order to have an answer choice fit the question, then you should move on and consider the other answer choices. These are normal problems rooted in reality. The applicable relationship or explanation may not be readily apparent, but it is there for you to figure out. Use your common sense to interpret anything that isn't clear.

Answer Choice Strategies

⊘ Answer Selection

The most thorough way to pick an answer choice is to identify and eliminate wrong answers until only one is left, then confirm it is the correct answer. Sometimes an answer choice may immediately seem right, but be careful. The test writers will usually put more than one reasonable answer choice on each question, so take a second to read all of them and make sure that the other choices are not equally obvious. As long as you have time left, it is better to read every answer choice than to pick the first one that looks right without checking the others.

⊘ Answer Choice Families

An answer choice family consists of two (in rare cases, three) answer choices that are very similar in construction and cannot all be true at the same time. If you see two answer choices that are direct opposites or parallels, one of them is usually the correct answer. For instance, if one answer choice says that quantity *x* increases and another either says that quantity *x* decreases (opposite) or says that quantity *y* increases (parallel), then those answer choices would fall into the same family. An answer choice that doesn't match the construction of the answer choice family is more likely to be incorrect. Most questions will not have answer choice families, but when they do appear, you should be prepared to recognize them.

⊘ Eliminate Answers

Eliminate answer choices as soon as you realize they are wrong, but make sure you consider all possibilities. If you are eliminating answer choices and realize that the last one you are left with is also wrong, don't panic. Start over and consider each choice again. There may be something you missed the first time that you will realize on the second pass.

⊘ Avoid Fact Traps

Don't be distracted by an answer choice that is factually true but doesn't answer the question. You are looking for the choice that answers the question. Stay focused on what the question is asking for so you don't accidentally pick an answer that is true but incorrect. Always go back to the question and make sure the answer choice you've selected actually answers the question and is not merely a true statement.

⊘ Extreme Statements

In general, you should avoid answers that put forth extreme actions as standard practice or proclaim controversial ideas as established fact. An answer choice that states the "process should be used in certain situations, if..." is much more likely to be correct than one that states the "process should be discontinued completely." The first is a calm rational statement and doesn't even make a definitive, uncompromising stance, using a hedge word *if* to provide wiggle room, whereas the second choice is far more extreme.

⊘ Benchmark

As you read through the answer choices and you come across one that seems to answer the question well, mentally select that answer choice. This is not your final answer, but it's the one that will help you evaluate the other answer choices. The one that you selected is your benchmark or standard for judging each of the other answer choices. Every other answer choice must be compared to your benchmark. That choice is correct until proven otherwise by another answer choice beating it. If you find a better answer, then that one becomes your new benchmark. Once you've decided that no other choice answers the question as well as your benchmark, you have your final answer.

⊘ Predict the Answer

Before you even start looking at the answer choices, it is often best to try to predict the answer. When you come up with the answer on your own, it is easier to avoid distractions and traps because you will know exactly what to look for. The right answer choice is unlikely to be word-for-word what you came up with, but it should be a close match. Even if you are confident that you have the right answer, you should still take the time to read each option before moving on.

General Strategies

⊘ Tough Questions

If you are stumped on a problem or it appears too hard or too difficult, don't waste time. Move on! Remember though, if you can quickly check for obviously incorrect answer choices, your chances of guessing correctly are greatly improved. Before you completely give up, at least try to knock out a couple of possible answers. Eliminate what you can and then guess at the remaining answer choices before moving on.

⊘ Check Your Work

Since you will probably not know every term listed and the answer to every question, it is important that you get credit for the ones that you do know. Don't miss any questions through careless mistakes. If at all possible, try to take a second to look back over your answer selection and make sure you've selected the correct answer choice and haven't made a costly careless mistake (such as marking an answer choice that you didn't mean to mark). This quick double check should more than pay for itself in caught mistakes for the time it costs.

⊘ Pace Yourself

It's easy to be overwhelmed when you're looking at a page full of questions; your mind is confused and full of random thoughts, and the clock is ticking down faster than you would like. Calm down and maintain the pace that you have set for yourself. Especially as you get down to the last few minutes of the test, don't let the small numbers on the clock make you panic. As long as you are on track by monitoring your pace, you are guaranteed to have time for each question.

⊘ Don't Rush

It is very easy to make errors when you are in a hurry. Maintaining a fast pace in answering questions is pointless if it makes you miss questions that you would have gotten right otherwise. Test writers like to include distracting information and wrong answers that seem right. Taking a little extra time to avoid careless mistakes can make all the difference in your test score. Find a pace that allows you to be confident in the answers that you select.

✓ Keep Moving

Panicking will not help you pass the test, so do your best to stay calm and keep moving. Taking deep breaths and going through the answer elimination steps you practiced can help to break through a stress barrier and keep your pace.

Final Notes

The combination of a solid foundation of content knowledge and the confidence that comes from practicing your plan for applying that knowledge is the key to maximizing your performance on test day. As your foundation of content knowledge is built up and strengthened, you'll find that the strategies included in this chapter become more and more effective in helping you quickly sift through the distractions and traps of the test to isolate the correct answer.

Now that you're preparing to move forward into the test content chapters of this book, be sure to keep your goal in mind. As you read, think about how you will be able to apply this information on the test. If you've already seen sample questions for the test and you have an idea of the question format and style, try to come up with questions of your own that you can answer based on what you're reading. This will give you valuable practice applying your knowledge in the same ways you can expect to on test day.

Good luck and good studying!

Mathematics

Number and Number Sense

Place Value

Numbers can be broken apart and composed based on their **place value**. For example, the number 129,548 can be expressed in **expanded form** as 100,000 + 20,000 + 9,000 + 500 + 40 + 8. You should also be comfortable going from expanded form to standard form. For example, what number is represented by 30,000 + 400 + 80 + 2? Notice 3 groups of ten-thousands, 0 groups of thousands, 4 groups of hundreds, 8 groups of tens, and 2 groups of ones. This becomes 30,482.

Sometimes you will be asked to compose and decompose numbers that are presented in **picture** or **model** form. This usually includes base-10 blocks. For example, consider the model below. How many groups of thousands, hundreds, tens, and ones are there? There is 1 group of 1,000, 2 groups of 100, 4 groups of 10, and 7 ones. This forms the number 1,247.

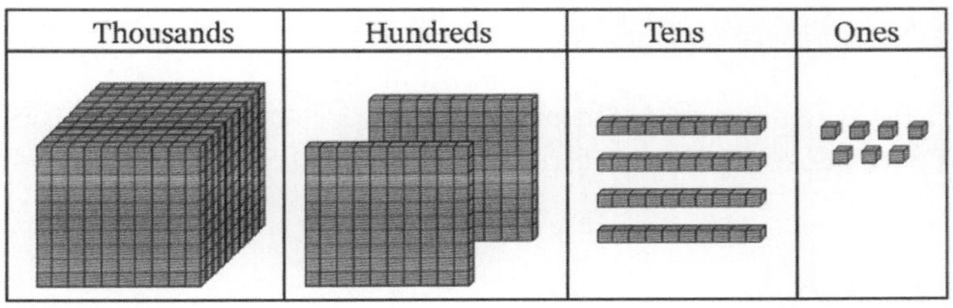

Example

Decompose the number 452,837 into expanded form.

The number 452,837 can be decomposed based on its place value. The 4 in the hundred-thousands place represents 400,000. The 5 in the ten-thousands place represents 50,000. The 2 in the thousands place represents 2,000. The 8 in the hundreds place represents 800. The 3 in the tens place represents 30. The 7 in the ones place represents 7. Altogether, 452,837 in expanded form is 400,000 + 50,000 + 2,000 + 800 + 30 + 7.

Example

What is the combined value of all of the base ten blocks below? Express the number in expanded form.

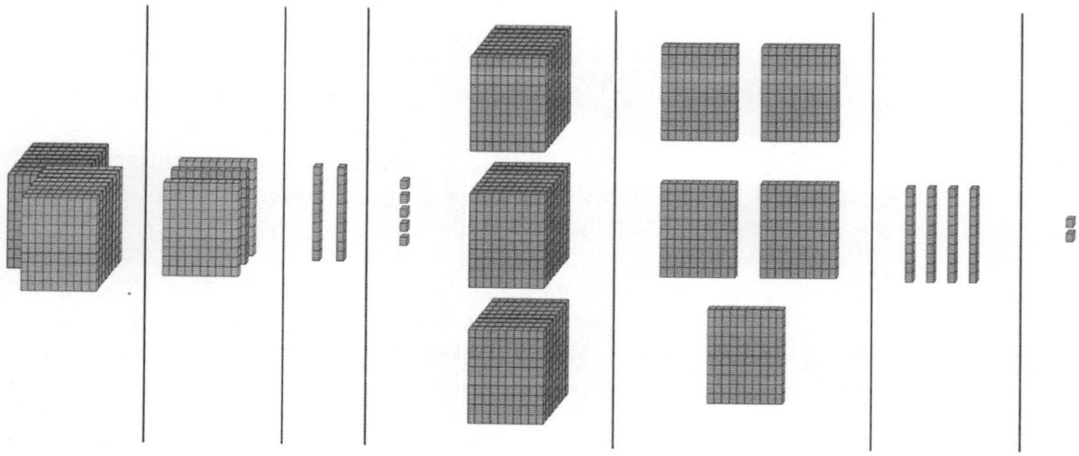

There are 5 blocks of 1,000. There are 8 plates of 100. There are 6 rods of 10. There are 7 cubes of 1. 5,000 + 800 + 60 + 7 represents the amount in expanded form. In standard form the value is 5,867.

The Base-10 Number System

Consider the numbers 3, 30, 300, and 3,000. What happens from one number to the next? Each number is **10 times** the previous number. The great thing about the **base-10 number system** is the **consistent pattern** regarding place value. As you move from left to right, place value increases by a factor of 10. As you noticed in the previous example, 30 is 10 times as large as 3, 300 is 10 times as large as 30, 3,000 is 10 times as large as 300. This concept can be applied when you jump from a small place value to a large place value. For example, consider 45 and 450,000. How do we get from 45 to 450,000?

$$45 \times 10 = 450$$

$$45 \times 100 = 4{,}500$$

$$45 \times 1{,}000 = 45{,}000$$

$$45 \times 10{,}000 = 450{,}000$$

The important thing to remember is that each place value increases by a factor of 10. Another way to think about this is $45 \times 10 \times 10 \times 10 \times 10 = 450{,}000$.

Review Video: Number Place Value
Visit mometrix.com/academy and enter code: 205433

ROUNDING

There are many ways to round numbers. For example, when the number 89 is rounded to the nearest ten it becomes 90. When 89 is rounded to the nearest hundred it becomes 100.

A **number line** is a great tool to use when **rounding** numbers.

When rounding to the nearest ten, set up a number line with intervals of 10. Plot the number on the number line and look for the multiple of 10 that the number is closest to. For example, notice how 18 is closer to 20 than to 10. This means that 18 rounded to the nearest ten is 20.

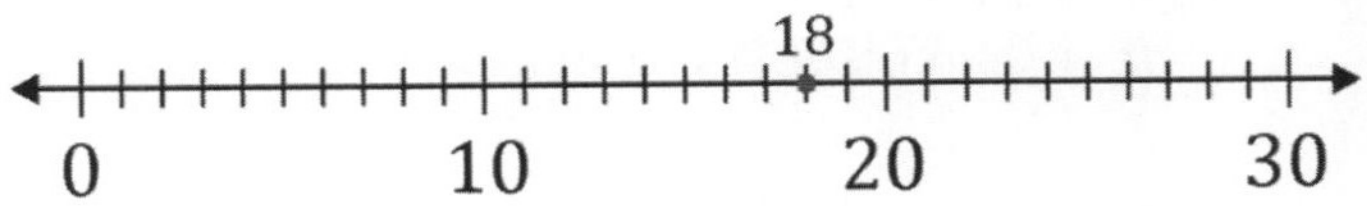

The same process works for numbers with larger place values. Consider the number 341. Create a number line with intervals of 100. Plot 341 on the number line. Notice that it is closer to 300 than 400. This means 341 rounded to the nearest hundred is 300.

Let's look at one more. Consider the number 1,627. Plot the point on a number line that has intervals of 1,000. Notice how 1,627 is closer to 2,000 than 1,000. This means that 1,627 rounded to the nearest thousand, which is 2,000.

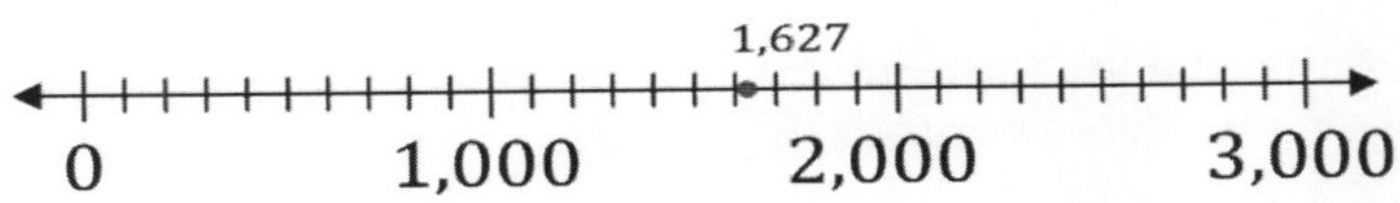

COMPARING NUMBERS

Two important symbols are the **inequality symbols** for **greater than** (>) and **less than** (<). For example, 45 > 35 means 45 is greater than 35, and 26 < 62 means 26 is less than 62. We can now build on this skill to compare and order whole numbers up to 100,000. The important thing to remember is place value. Remember, when comparing numbers, start by comparing the **farthest left digit**. For example, when comparing 452,987 and 455,798, start by comparing the hundred-thousands place.

$\underline{4}52,987$ and $\underline{4}55,798$

In this case, both values are 4. Since they are the same, move to the ten-thousands place.

$4\underline{5}2,987$ and $4\underline{5}5,798$

Both values are both 5, so move to the thousands place.

$45\underline{2},987$ and $45\underline{5},798$

2 is less than 5, so 452,987 is less than 455,798.

This can be expressed using an inequality symbol: 452,987 < 455,798.

EXAMPLE

Order the three values from least to greatest using the symbols < and >:

65,033; 65,300; 65,030.

When comparing numbers, start with the farthest left digit and move right until the digits differ. All three numbers have the same digit in the ten-thousands place (6). Move right. All three numbers have the same digit in the thousands place (5). Move right. 65,300 has the largest digit in the hundreds place (3), therefore it is the largest number. Move right. Two numbers remain. Both 65,030 and 65,033 have the same digit in the tens place (3). Move right. 65,033 has a larger digit in the ones place, therefore it is larger than 65,030. The numbers from least to greatest are 65,030 < 65,033 < 65,300.

EXAMPLE

Use an inequality symbol to compare 905,532 and 905,600.

Compare the numbers by comparing each digit from left to right. The digits in the hundred-thousands, ten-thousands, and thousands place are all the same (905). Keep moving right. The hundreds digits differ. One says 6 and one says 5. This means that 905,600 is larger than 905,532. 905,600 > 905,532, or 905,532 < 905,600.

FRACTIONS

Values that are greater than 0 but less than or equal to 1 can be represented as a **fraction**. For example, the pizza, watermelon, and lemon are each sliced into equal pieces. The pizza has 6 equal pieces, the watermelon has 4 equal pieces, and the lemon has 8 equal pieces. These values represent the denominator of a fraction. Remember, the **denominator** is the bottom number in a fraction, which represents the **total number of pieces**.

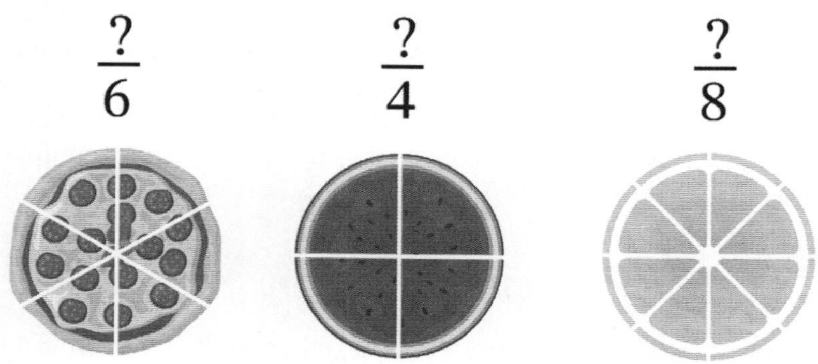

If 3 slices of each food are eaten, 3 would be the **numerator**.

$\frac{3}{6}$ of the pizza is eaten. $\frac{3}{4}$ of the watermelon is eaten. $\frac{3}{8}$ of the lemon is eaten.

Fractions can also be modeled using number lines or **fraction strips**.

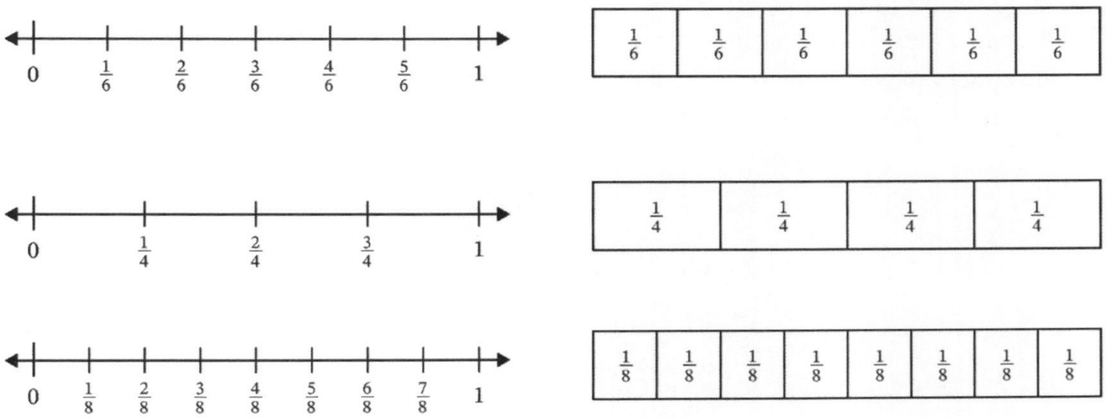

FRACTIONS AND NUMBER LINES

Fractions are often displayed using models, fraction strips, pictures, or number lines. When determining a fraction from a number line, check to see how many **parts** there are within **one whole**. For example, consider the number line below. Notice how there are 4 **equal parts** from 0 to 1. This means each hash mark represents 1 out of 4, or $\frac{1}{4}$. Count up by $\frac{1}{4}$ to determine the missing value. $\frac{1}{4}, \frac{2}{4}, \frac{3}{4}$... The missing value is $\frac{3}{4}$.

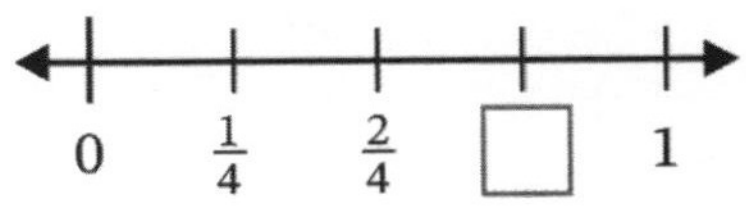

Consider the number line below. To identify the fraction that the green dot represents, first figure out the interval. The **interval** is essentially how many equal parts are shown to be within one whole number. In this case, there are 10 equal parts from 0 to 1. This means the interval is tenths. Starting from 0, or $\frac{0}{10}$, each hop to the right increases by $\frac{1}{10}$. The dot represents 8 hops, so $\frac{8}{10}$.

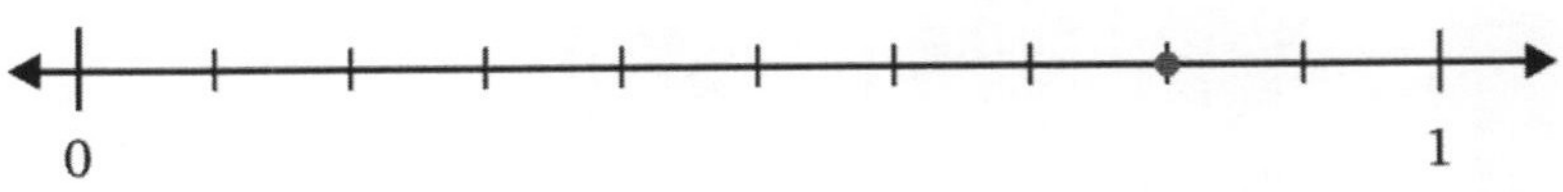

Unit Fractions

A **unit fraction** represents **one part** out of the whole. For example, $\frac{1}{2}$, $\frac{1}{4}$, $\frac{1}{6}$ and $\frac{1}{10}$ are all considered unit fractions. If the **numerator** is **1**, then the fraction is considered a unit fraction. Unit fractions can be shown in a model. For example, if a pan of brownies is cut into 8 equal pieces and 1 brownie is eaten, the consumed brownie represents the unit fraction $\frac{1}{8}$. The numerator is 1, and the denominator represents the total number of parts.

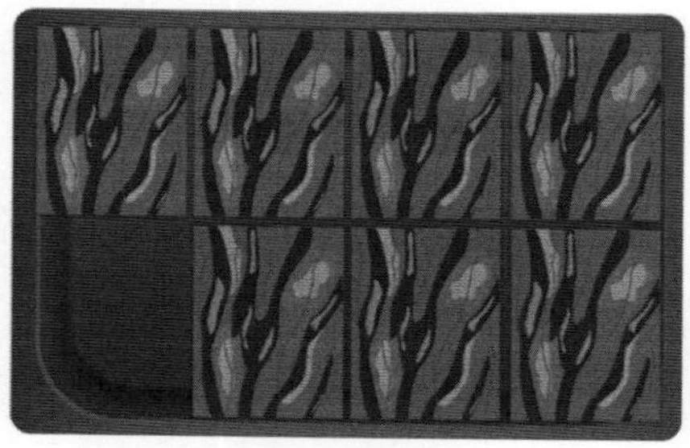

Composing and Decomposing Fractions

Fractions can be thought of as a **collection** of unit fractions. For example, the fraction $\frac{4}{5}$ is composed of $\frac{1}{5}+\frac{1}{5}+\frac{1}{5}+\frac{1}{5}$. The opposite of **composing** a fraction is **decomposing** a fraction. When a fraction is **broken up** into the sum of its unit fractions, it has been decomposed. For example, $\frac{6}{8}$ can be decomposed into $\frac{1}{8}+\frac{1}{8}+\frac{1}{8}+\frac{1}{8}+\frac{1}{8}+\frac{1}{8}$.

Using Models to Solve Problems Involving Fractions

Fractions represent part of a whole. One helpful way to see this is to draw a model. For example, if a cake is sliced into 8 equal slices, we can model the scenario by drawing lines to divide the cake into 8 slices. If 4 slices are eaten, then $\frac{4}{8}$ remain.

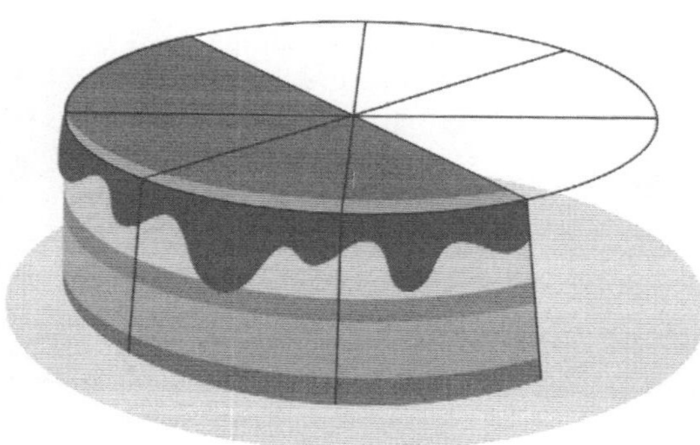

What if a cake had 10 slices, and each person wanted 2 slices? How many people could this cake feed?

Draw a quick picture of a cake sliced into 10 pieces. How many groups of 2 slices are there? A cake with 10 slices has 5 groups of 2. This cake would feed 5 people.

Drawing a quick sketch is often a helpful strategy for problems involving equal pieces.

EXAMPLE

Use the fraction strips to identify an equivalent fraction to $\frac{2}{3}$.

$\frac{1}{2}$	$\frac{1}{2}$				
$\frac{1}{3}$	$\frac{1}{3}$	$\frac{1}{3}$			
$\frac{1}{4}$	$\frac{1}{4}$	$\frac{1}{4}$	$\frac{1}{4}$		
$\frac{1}{5}$	$\frac{1}{5}$	$\frac{1}{5}$	$\frac{1}{5}$	$\frac{1}{5}$	
$\frac{1}{6}$	$\frac{1}{6}$	$\frac{1}{6}$	$\frac{1}{6}$	$\frac{1}{6}$	$\frac{1}{6}$

Locate the fraction strips for $\frac{1}{3}$. Move to the right to locate $\frac{2}{3}$. Notice how $\frac{2}{3}$ is the same length as $\frac{4}{6}$. The fractions $\frac{2}{3}$ and $\frac{4}{6}$ are considered equivalent fractions. $\frac{4}{6}$ is the correct answer.

EXAMPLE

Use the fraction number lines to identify three fractions that are equivalent to $\frac{4}{8}$.

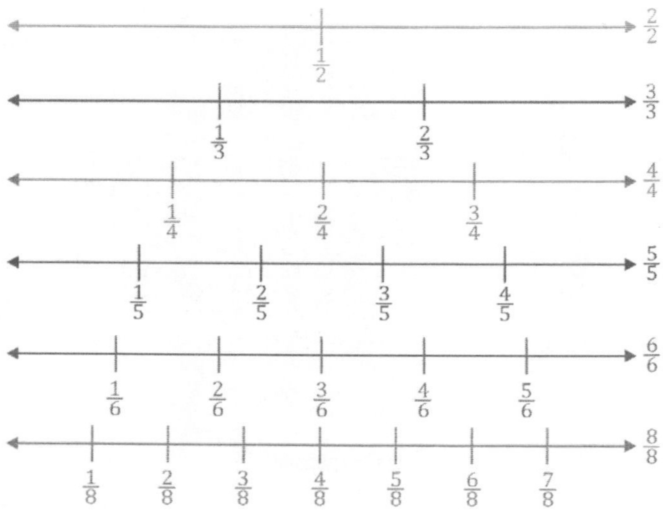

Equivalent fractions represent the same distance from 0 on a number line. Locate the fraction $\frac{4}{8}$. Compare this distance with the other number lines. Notice how the red, blue, and orange number lines have values at the same distance. The fractions $\frac{1}{2}$, $\frac{2}{4}$, and $\frac{3}{6}$ are the same distance from 0 as $\frac{4}{8}$. This means $\frac{1}{2}$, $\frac{2}{4}$, $\frac{3}{6}$, and $\frac{4}{8}$ are all equivalent fractions. The answer is $\frac{1}{2}$, $\frac{2}{4}$, $\frac{3}{6}$.

EQUIVALENT FRACTIONS

Equivalent fractions are fractions that represent the **same amount**. For example, $\frac{1}{2}$ of a pizza is the same amount as $\frac{2}{4}$ of a pizza. It can be helpful to show equivalent fractions on a number line.

Consider the number lines below. Each number line extends from 0 to 1, and all of the number lines are the same length.

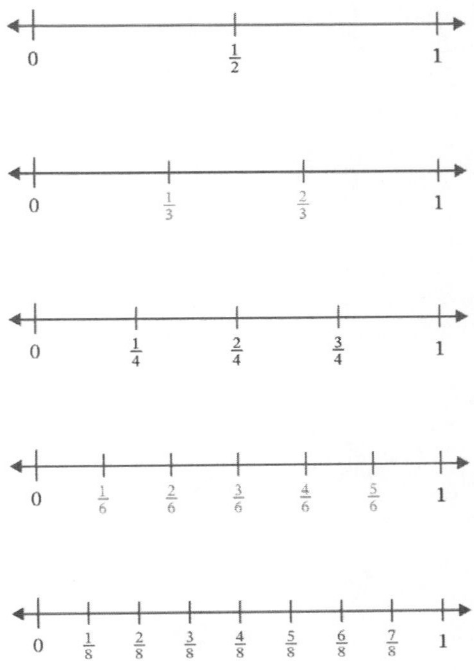

Notice how the distance at $\frac{1}{2}$ is the same distance as $\frac{2}{4}$, $\frac{3}{6}$, and $\frac{4}{8}$. These are all considered equivalent fractions because they all represent the same amount. $\frac{1}{2}$, $\frac{2}{4}$, $\frac{3}{6}$, and $\frac{4}{8}$ are all the same distance from 0 on the number line.

The same concept can be seen using a model. The circle below is made up of 3 equal parts. One part is shaded. This shaded part represents $\frac{1}{3}$. What is another fraction equivalent to $\frac{1}{3}$?

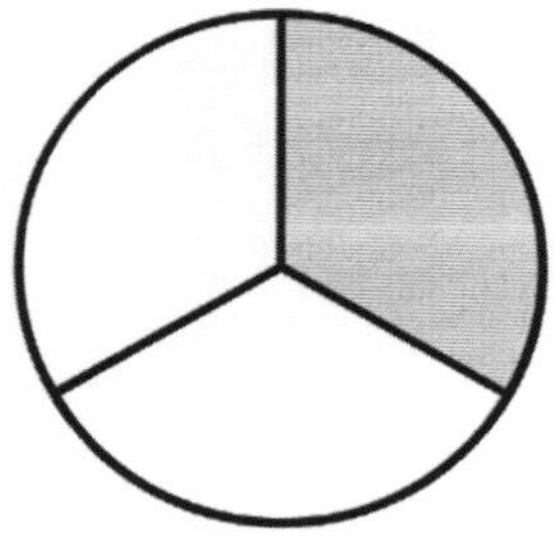

Instead of dividing the circle into 3 equal parts, divide it into 6 equal parts. Notice how 1 out of 3 becomes 2 out of 6. The fraction $\frac{2}{6}$ is equivalent to $\frac{1}{3}$.

Remember, the term **equivalent** means the same amount. It can be helpful to find equivalent fractions using a number line. Fractions that are the same distance from 0 on a number line are considered equivalent fractions. Notice how the two red points on the number lines below are the same distance from 0. The fractions $\frac{1}{3}$ and $\frac{2}{6}$ represent the same distance, therefore they are equivalent. Are there any other pairs of equivalent fractions visible on the number lines below?

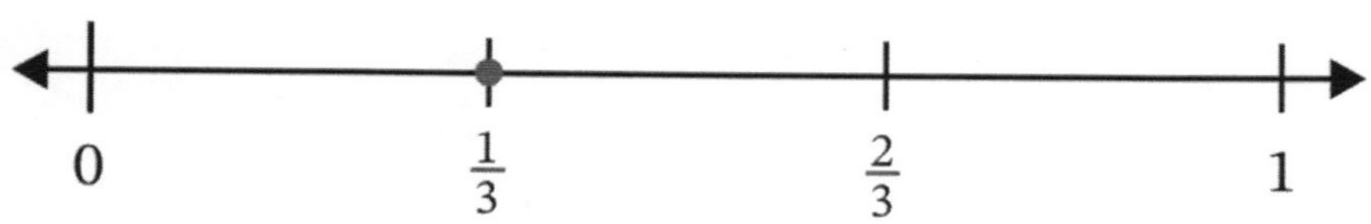

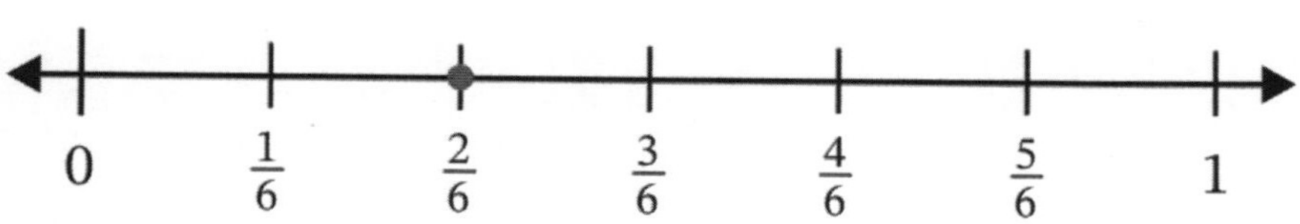

Yes! $\frac{2}{3}$ and $\frac{4}{6}$ are the same distance from 0. $\frac{2}{3}$ and $\frac{4}{6}$ are equivalent fractions.

Equivalent fractions can also be determined using an area model. Consider the fraction $\frac{1}{2}$. The area model shows a rectangle with 2 equal pieces, and 1 part shaded. This represents $\frac{1}{2}$. What is another way to express $\frac{1}{2}$? In other words, what is an equivalent fraction?

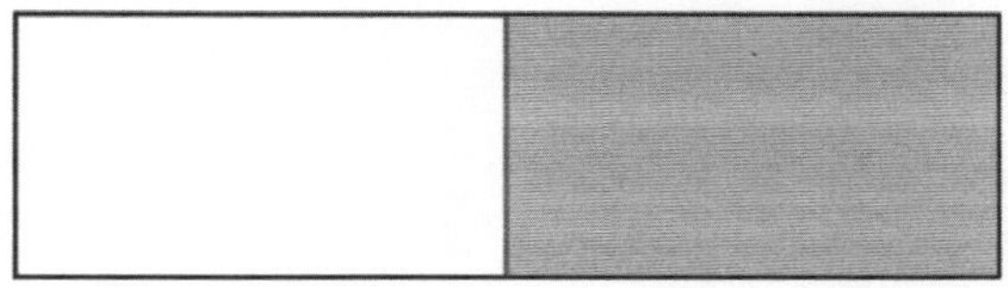

What if the same rectangle was sliced into 8 equal pieces? How many pieces would be shaded?

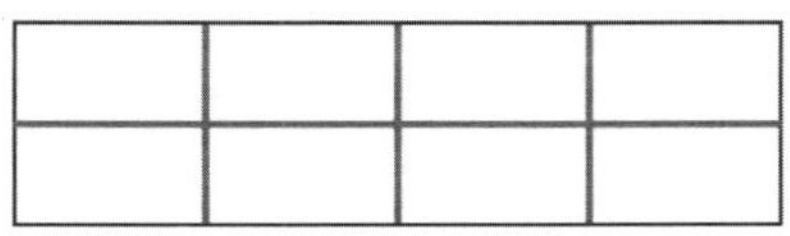

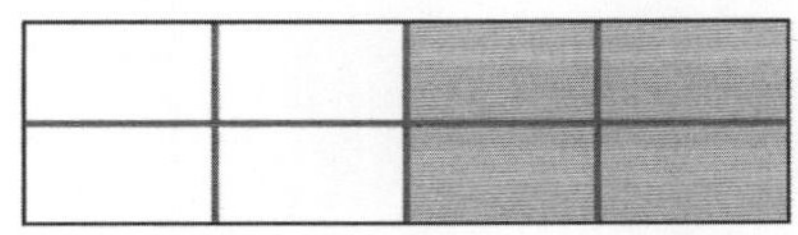

When the model is sliced into 8 equal pieces, 4 parts are shaded. $\frac{1}{2}$ and $\frac{4}{8}$ are considered equivalent fractions.

Comparing Fractions

Many fractions can be compared using logic. For example, consider the unit fractions $\frac{1}{4}$ and $\frac{1}{3}$. These fractions could be compared using a number line or by drawing a picture. However, these tools are not always necessary.

Both fractions are unit fractions, so they represent one part out of the total. $\frac{1}{4}$ represents one of the fourths. $\frac{1}{3}$ represents one of the thirds. Thirds are larger than fourths, so $\frac{1}{3}$ is larger than $\frac{1}{4}$.

The numerators are the same, and thirds are larger than fourths: $\frac{1}{3} > \frac{1}{4}$.

Now consider two fractions that have the same denominator. Compare the two fractions $\frac{2}{4}$ and $\frac{3}{4}$. Again, a picture or number line is not always necessary.

Both fractions have 4 in the denominator. This means both fractions have a whole of 4. However, 2 parts out of 4 is less than 3 parts out of 4. Think: 2 pieces are less than 3 pieces, so $\frac{2}{4}$ is less than $\frac{3}{4}$: $\frac{2}{4} < \frac{3}{4}$.

Example

Use an inequality symbol to compare the two fractions $\frac{4}{5}$ and $\frac{4}{6}$.

The numerator of a fraction represents the "parts". The denominator of a fraction represents the "whole". The fractions $\frac{4}{5}$ and $\frac{4}{6}$ have the same number of parts but a different number of total parts.

Fifths are larger than sixths. Therefore, 4 out of 5 is more than 4 out of 6. Think about it this way: 4 large pieces is more than 4 small pieces.

Notice how 4 pieces out of 5 is more than 4 pieces out of 6.

$$\frac{4}{5} > \frac{4}{6}$$

EXAMPLE

Use an inequality symbol to compare the two fractions: $\frac{3}{8}$ and $\frac{2}{8}$.

Both fractions have the same denominator. $\frac{3}{8}$ and $\frac{2}{8}$ both have 8 total parts. 3 out of 8 parts is more than 2 out of 8 parts. This means that $\frac{3}{8}$ is greater than $\frac{2}{8}$.

Notice how 3 pieces out of 8 is more than 2 pieces out of 8.

$$\frac{3}{8} > \frac{2}{8}$$

Computation and Estimation

Solving Problems

Estimating Solutions

Estimating sums and differences is a way to come up with an answer that is close to the exact answer. For example, if you run 9 miles each week for 7 weeks, how many total miles have you run? 9 rounded to the nearest 10 is 10. 7 groups of 10 is 70. You have run about 70 miles. This is close to the actual answer, which is 63 miles.

Compatible numbers make addition and subtraction easier. **Compatible numbers** are numbers that make addition or subtraction easier to do, and often they end in a 0 or 5. Instead of calculating 257 − 49, consider using compatible numbers. 257 is close to 250, and 49 is close to 50, and 250 − 50 are compatible because they can be quickly subtracted: 250 − 50 = 200. This is close to the actual answer of 257 − 49 = 208.

Rounding

Rounding is another strategy that saves time when adding and subtracting. If the digit to the right is 5 or greater, then the rounded number will **round** up. If the digit to the right is less than 5, then the rounded number stays the same.

Round 248 to the nearest 10.

248: 4 is in the tens place. The digit to the right of the 4 will indicate whether the 4 stays the same or rounds up to 5. To the right of 4 there is an 8. This means the 4 will round up to 5. 248 becomes 250 when rounded to the nearest 10.

Round 248 to the nearest 100.

248: 2 is in the hundreds place. The digit to the right of the 2 will indicate whether the 2 stays the same or rounds up to 3. To the right of 2 there is a 4. This means the 2 will stay the same. 248 becomes 200 when rounded to the nearest hundred.

Rounding to the nearest ten or hundred can sometimes make addition or subtraction problems easier.

For example, use rounding to estimate the sum of 49 and 253. If 49 is rounded to the nearest ten, it becomes 50. If 253 is rounded to the nearest ten, it becomes 250. Now, add 50 and 250: 50 + 250 = 300. In this case, rounding made the addition much simpler and is still close to the actual answer of 302.

Place Value Strategy

One- and two-step **addition and subtraction problems** can be solved using place value. For example, 432 + 826 can be thought of as a group of 4 hundreds, 3 tens, and 2 ones, plus 8 hundreds, 2 tens, and 6 ones. Combine the place values to solve:

$$4 \text{ hundreds} + 8 \text{ hundreds} = 12 \text{ hundreds}$$

$$3 \text{ tens} + 2 \text{ tens} = 5 \text{ tens}$$

$$2 \text{ ones} + 6 \text{ ones} = 8 \text{ ones}$$

$$1{,}200 + 50 + 8 = 1{,}258$$

Two-Step Problems

Consider the scenario: A shopper starts with \$456 in their wallet and then spends \$128 on shoes. Later that day, the shopper finds a 20-dollar bill in their pocket. Altogether, how much money does the shopper have left after shoe shopping?

The scenario can be solved in two steps. The shopper starts with \$456 and then spends \$128. This means that \$128 have been subtracted from \$456. \$456 consists of 4 hundreds, 5 tens, and 6 ones. \$128 consists of 1 hundred, 2 tens, and 8 ones. 8 ones cannot be subtracted from 6 ones, which means **regrouping** needs to occur.

4 hundreds, 5 tens, and 6 ones becomes 4 hundreds, 4 tens, and 16 ones. Now subtraction can continue: $456 - 128 = 328$.

$$\begin{array}{r} 4\;5\;6 \\ -\;1\;2\;8 \\ \hline \end{array} \quad \rightarrow \quad \begin{array}{r} {\scriptstyle 4\;16} \\ 4\;\not{5}\;\not{6} \\ -\;1\;2\;8 \\ \hline 3\;2\;8 \end{array}$$

The shopper then finds \$20 in their pocket. This indicates adding 20: $328 + 20 = 348$.

The shopper has \$348 after shoe shopping.

<u>Example</u>

Find the value of the expression below:

$$(648 + 250) - 30$$

648 consists of 6 hundreds, 4 tens, and 8 ones. 250 consists of 2 hundreds, 5 tens, and 0 ones. Combine each place value to find the sum.

$$600 + 200 + 40 + 50 + 8 + 0 = 898$$

Now, subtract 30, which consists of 3 tens, from 898. 898 consists of 9 tens. Subtract 3 tens from this: $898 - 30 = 868$.

$$(648 + 250) - 30 = 868$$

The answer is 868.

<u>Example</u>

Find the value of the expression below:

$$640 - 180$$

Think about 640 and 180 in terms of place value.

$$640 = 6 \text{ hundreds} + 4 \text{ tens} + 0 \text{ ones}$$

$$180 = 1 \text{ hundred} + 8 \text{ tens} + 0 \text{ ones}$$

640 has 4 tens, which is not enough to subtract 8 tens from.

Regrouping is necessary. 1 of the hundreds becomes 10 tens. So, 6 hundreds + 4 tens + 0 ones becomes 5 hundreds + 14 tens + 0 ones.

Now subtraction can begin.

(5 hundreds + 14 tens + 0 ones) − (1 hundred + 8 tens + 0 ones) becomes

4 hundreds + 6 tens + 0 ones. In standard form, this is 460.

$$640 - 180 = 460$$

The answer is 460.

Pictures and Models

Use base ten blocks to represent 185 taken from 2 groups of 450 to get 715.

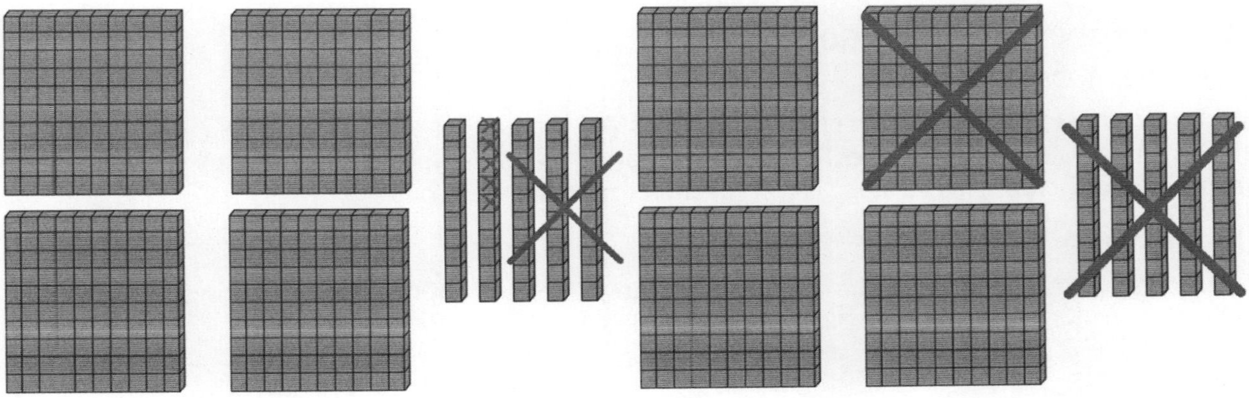

Number Lines

Make two jumps of 450, then back 185.

$$(450 + 450) - 185 = 715$$

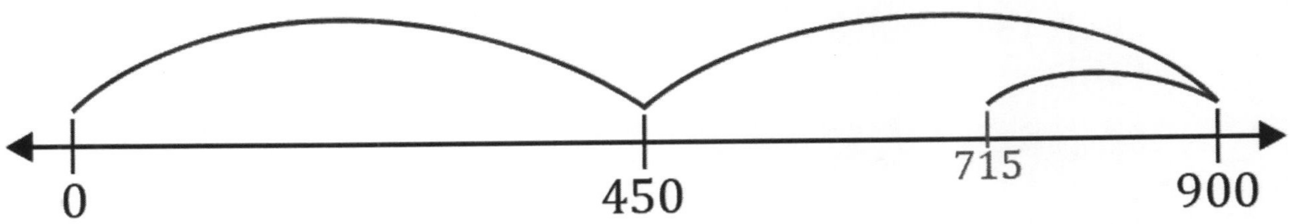

Equations

$$m = (450 + 450) - 185$$

The equation simplifies to $m = 715$, or $715.

Example

Use the number line to represent 200 + 50 − 125.

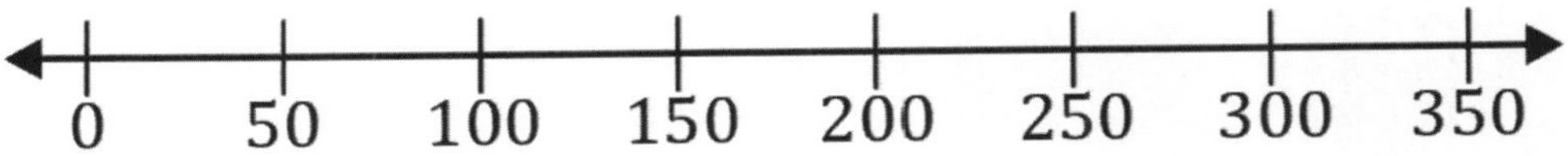

Start by adding 50 to 200. Make one jump forward from 200 to 250.

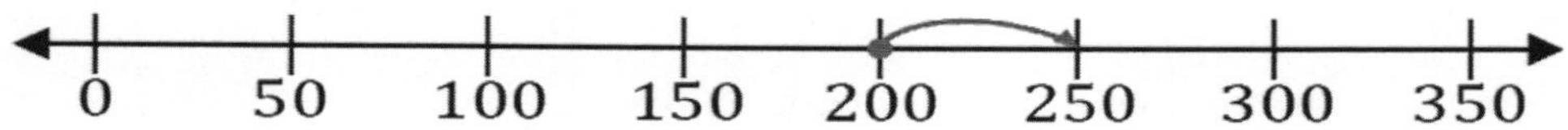

Now subtract 125. Jump back 100 and then back 25 more. 250 becomes 150 and then 125.

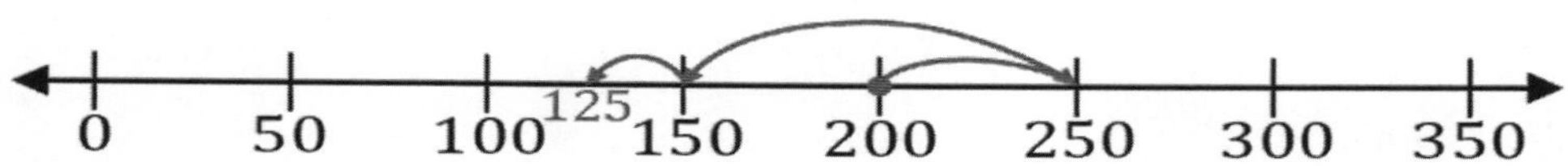

$$200 + 50 - 125 = 125.$$

REPRESENTING MULTIPLICATION

REPEATED ADDITION

Multiplication is the process of counting equally sized groups. 5 groups of 7 means $7 + 7 + 7 + 7 + 7$. 5 groups of 7 is 35. The process of using addition to solve multiplication problems is known as **repeated addition**. This strategy is a great choice in many scenarios.

NUMBER LINES

A number line can be used to show repeated addition. The **number line** below shows 4 equal hops of 3. 4 hops of 3 represents 4×3, which is 12: $3 + 3 + 3 + 3 = 12$.

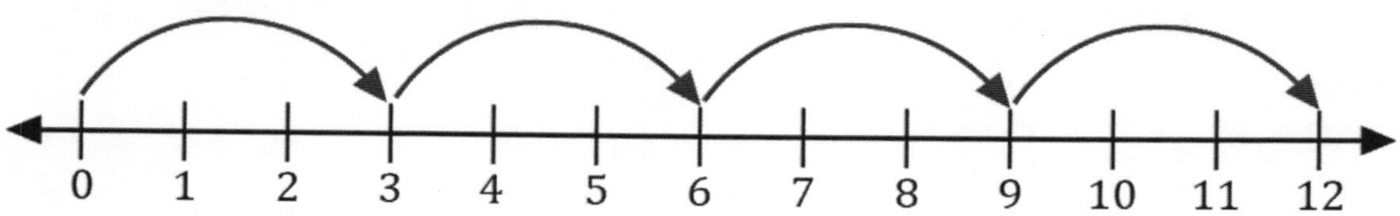

ARRAYS

An array is a collection and rows and columns representing a multiplication problem. This **array** has 10 columns and 4 rows. This array represents $10 \times 4 = 40$.

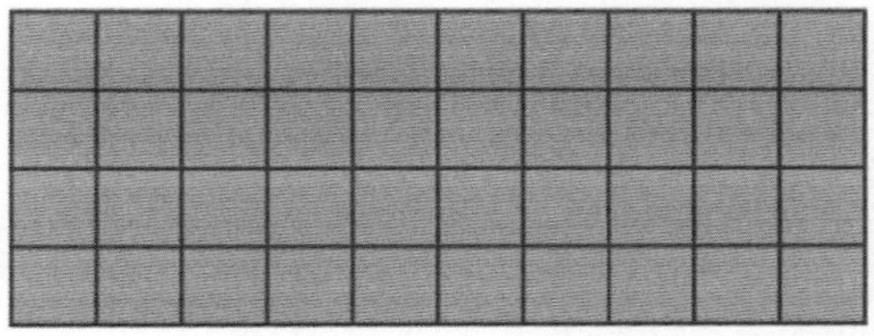

2 rows of 2 columns: $2 \times 2 = 4$

3 rows of 5 columns: $3 \times 5 = 15$

4 rows of 4 columns: $4 \times 4 = 16$

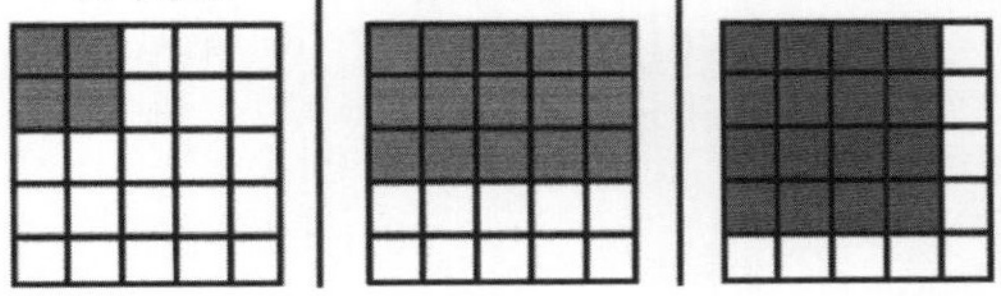

An **array** can be useful when solving real-world multiplication problems. For example, if a total of 7 blue fish are swimming in 3 separate groups, how many fish are there total?

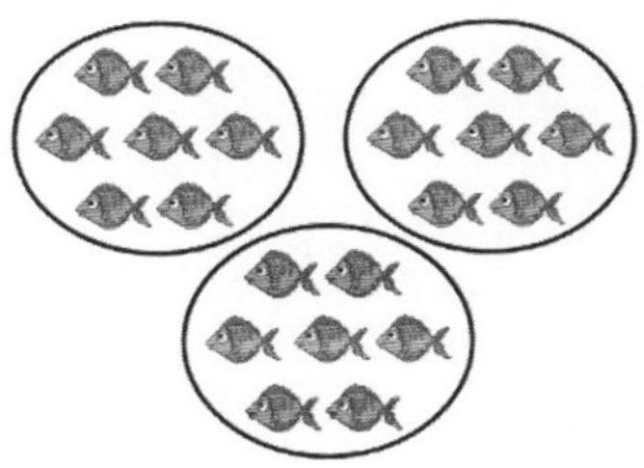

Drawing 3 groups of 7 is similar to creating an array of 3×7. Instead of creating 3 rows of 7 columns, the fish can be arranged into groups with 7 fish in each group. The total number of fish can be added up to find that $3 \times 7 = 21$.

RECALLING MULTIPLICATION FACTS

It is a great accomplishment to memorize the multiplication and division facts from 0 to 10. This is a goal that can take some time, so keep practicing!

Some strategies that can help:

1. **Skip count by the larger number.** For example, for the problem 8×3 skip count by 8s not 3s. This can save some time. $8 + 8 + 8$ is quicker than $3 + 3 + 3 + 3 + 3 + 3 + 3 + 3$.
2. **Use facts that you do know to help you.** For example, if you are stuck on 7×4 but you know 5×7 is 35, use logic to help you. 5 groups of 7 is 7 more than 4 groups of 7, so subtract 7 from 35 to solve 4×7.

3. **Use multiplication to help with division.** Multiplication and division are inverse operations. This means they undo each other. For example, $9 \times 4 = 36$ and $4 \times 9 = 36$ represent the inverse of $36 \div 4 = 9$ and $36 \div 9 = 4$. Your multiplication facts and division facts go hand-in-hand! Remember, multiplication and division fact families use the same three numbers. For example, $8 \times 7 = 56$, $7 \times 8 = 56$, $56 \div 7 = 8$, and $56 \div 8 = 7$ all use the same three numbers.

STRATEGIES FOR MULTIPLICATION

Strategies such as mental math, skip counting, and drawing a model are great for single digit multiplication problems. However, for larger numbers, these strategies are less ideal. For example, solving 7×82 by skip counting would take quite a long time. 7, 14, 21, 28... all the way up to 574! Luckily, there are faster strategies for multiplying by two-digit numbers.

STANDARD ALGORITHM

Place the two-digit number over the one-digit number. Start by multiplying the numbers in the ones place: $2 \times 7 = 14$. Regroup the 14 into 1 and 4, as shown.

Now multiply 7 by the number in the tens place: $7 \times 8 = 56$. Add the 1 from up above: $56 + 1 = 57$. Write 57 down below: $82 \times 7 = 574$.

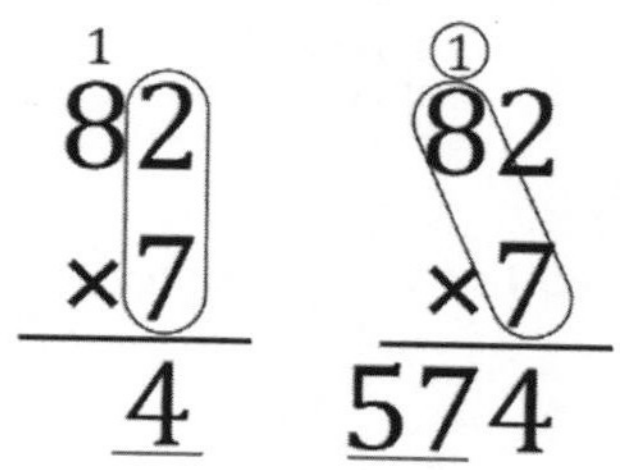

$82 \times 7 = 574$

PARTIAL PRODUCTS

Think about the two-digit number in terms of its place value.

82 consists of 8 tens and 2 ones: $82 = 80 + 2$.

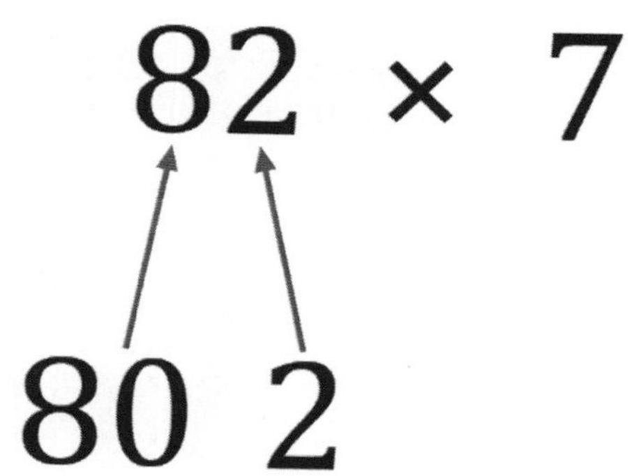

Now multiply each part by 7.

$$80 \times 7 = 560$$

$$2 \times 7 = 14$$

Now add the products.

$$\begin{array}{r} 560 \\ +\ \ 14 \\ \hline 574 \end{array}$$

$$560 + 14 = 574$$

Distributive Property

Using the **distribute property** is very similar to using **partial products**.

Distribute the 7 to each part of 82. 7×80 and 7×2.

$$7 \times 82$$

$$(7 \times 80) + (7 \times 2)$$

$$(7 \times 80) + (7 \times 2) = 560 + 14 = 574$$

Commutative Property

The **order** of the **factors** does not matter in multiplication.

$$3 \times 9 \times 4 = 4 \times 9 \times 3$$

Associative Property

In multiplication, the **arrangement** of **grouping symbols** does not affect the outcome.

$$(4 \times 9) \times 3 = 4 \times (9 \times 3)$$

Equal Groups

When a set of numbers are partitioned, or divided, into equal pieces, multiplication and division will be involved. For example, consider the following scenario:

There are 28 kids at a bowling party, and there are 7 lanes available. How many bowlers will be in each lane?

This kind of problem can be solved using a variety of strategies.

Solve Using a Picture or Model

Draw a quick sketch of 7 bowling lanes. There are 28 bowlers, so fill each lane one by one. Each lane holds 4 bowlers.

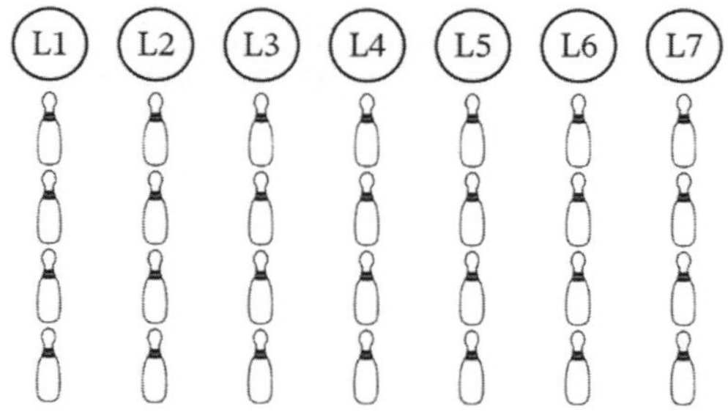

Solve Using Multiplication

7 groups of what equals 28? In other words, $7 \times ? = 28$.

$$7 \times 1 = 7$$

$$7 \times 2 = 14$$

$$7 \times 3 = 21$$

$$7 \times 4 = 28$$

Each lane will hold 4 bowlers.

Solve Using Division

$$28 \div 7 = ?$$

28 separated into 7 equal groups leaves 4 in each group.

$$28 \div 7 = 4$$

Even and Odd Numbers

You can determine if a number is even or odd by looking at the **ones** digit. Remember, the ones digit is the farthest digit to the right. If the ones digit can be divided, or is divisible, by 2, then the entire number is **even**. If the ones digit is not divisible by 2, then the entire number is **odd**. A number is divisible by 2 if it can be split into two groups without any remainders. For example, consider the number 3,916. The number 6 is in the ones place, and 6 is divisible by 2. Since the ones digit is divisible by 2, the number 3,916 is even. However, a number such as 83,097 is odd because the ones digit is 7, and 7 is not divisible by 2.

NUMBERS DIVISIBLE BY 2

One way to determine if a number is divisible by 2 is to create a quick sketch or model. For example, consider the number 845,029. In this case, the ones digit is 9. Create a sketch with two groups and see if 9 can be divided into two groups with no remainders.

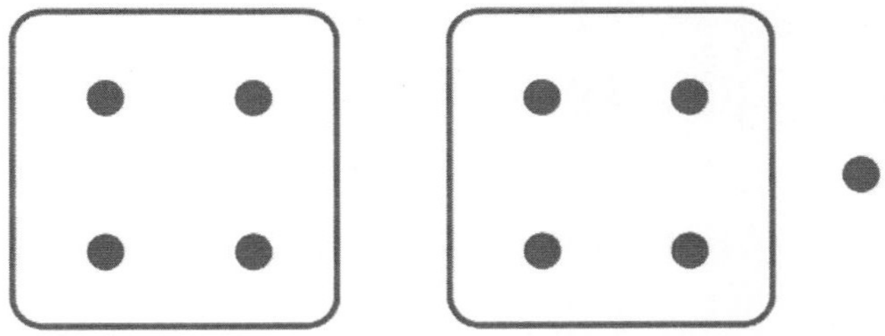

Notice that 9 cannot be split into two equal groups. It is close, but there is a remainder of 1. This means the number 845,029 is odd.

Now, consider the number 79,208. The ones digit is 8. The number 8 can be split into two equal groups, so 8 is divisible by 2. Therefore, 79,208 is even.

QUOTIENTS

Multiplication can be used to determine a **quotient**. Similar to addition and subtraction, multiplication and division are **inverse operations**. For example, $72 \div 9$ can be solved using the multiplication facts for 9. $72 \div 9 = ?$ Ask the question, "9 groups of what equals 72?"

$9 \times 6 = 54 \ldots 9 \times 7 = 63 \ldots 9 \times 8 = 72$. The missing number is 8. This means $72 \div 9 = 8$. This strategy is quite helpful because once the multiplication facts are automatic, division facts become automatic as well.

Consider the following examples:

$42 \div 7 = ?$ "7 groups of what equals 42?" $6 \times 7 = 42$. The product of 6 and 7 is 42. The quotient of 42 and 7 is 6.

$$42 \div 7 = 6$$

$48 \div 8 = ?$ "8 groups of what equals 48?" $6 \times 8 = 48$. The product of 6 and 8 is 48. The quotient of 48 and 8 is 6.

$$48 \div 8 = 6$$

SOLVING MULTIPLICATION AND DIVISION PROBLEMS

Multiplication and division can be **modeled** in many ways. Consider the problem 6×3. This can be solved using strategies such as **repeated addition**, **fact families**, **equal groups**, an **array**, **skip counting**, or a **tape diagram**. There are many options to choose from!

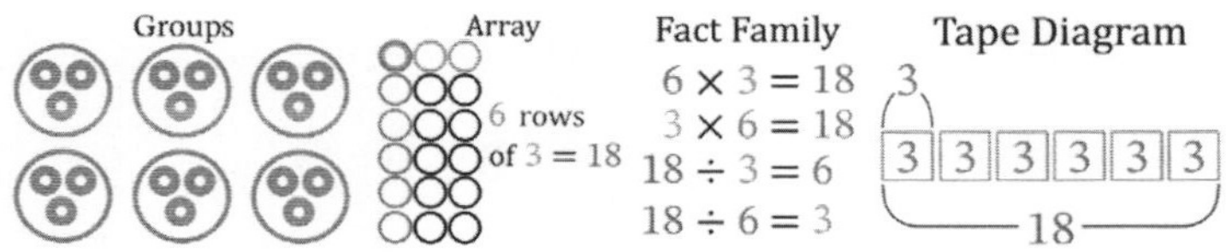

Skip Counting

3, 6, 9, 12, 15, 18

Repeated Addition

$3 + 3 + 3 + 3 + 3 + 3 = 18$

Two-step problems can be solved using the same strategies. Over time, these strategies will be replaced by memory.

EXAMPLE

Write a multiplication sentence that matches the tape diagram below.

4	4	4

The model shows 3 groups of 4. This can be expressed as the multiplication sentence $3 \times 4 = 12$.

EXAMPLE

Draw a model to represent $(15 \times 3) \div 5$.

The model shows 3 groups of 15, which equals 45.

45 is then divided into 5 equal groups. Each group contains 9 units.

$$(15 \times 3) \div 5 = 9$$

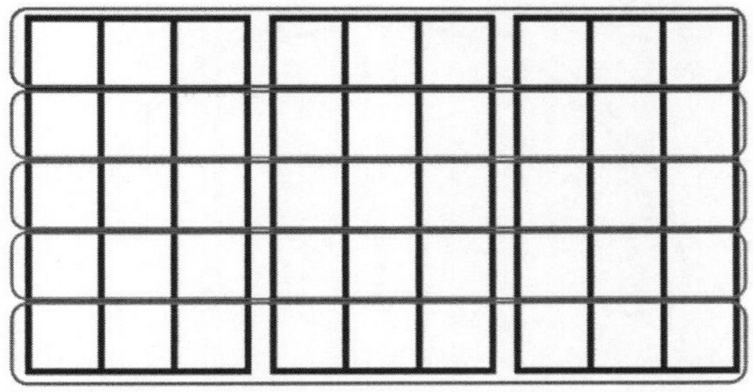

One-Step Problems

A rancher has 12 acres of farmland, and 8 sheep live on each acre. How many sheep does the rancher have in all?

This problem can be solved in one step. Think about it as a picture or a model. There are 12 acres, and each acre contains 8 sheep. 12 groups of 8 means 12×8. To find 12×8, break it down into $(10 \times 8) + (2 \times 8)$ and then $(80) + (16) = 96$. The rancher has 96 sheep.

Now, try a two-step problem. This time, consider using a picture or a model to solve.

Two-Step Problems

A florist is creating flower arrangements for an event. 72 bouquets can be arranged in 3 hours. How many bouquets can be arranged in 15 minutes?

72 bouquets divided into 3 hours means 24 bouquets in each hour.

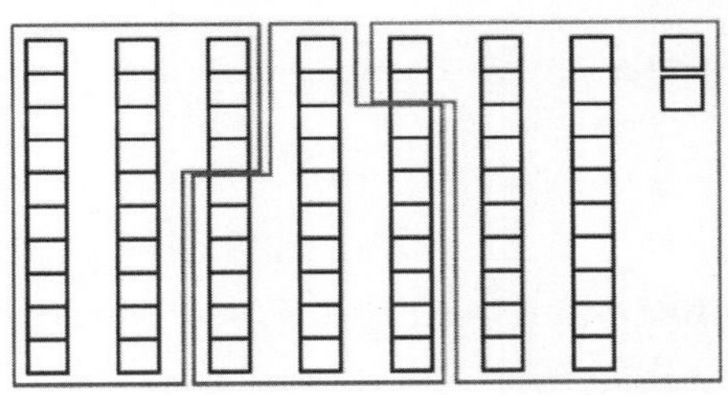

15 minutes is $\frac{1}{4}$ of an hour. We can see this by looking at a clock. The minute hand of a clock at 12:15 is $\frac{1}{4}$ through the circle.

So, divide 24 by 4.

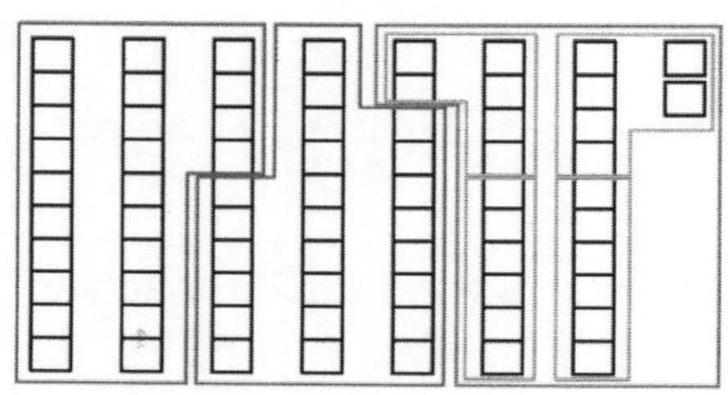

$$24 \div 4 = 6$$

So, 6 bouquets can be made every 15 minutes.

FRACTIONS

UNIT FRACTIONS

A **unit fraction** is any fraction with a numerator of 1. For example, $\frac{1}{2}, \frac{1}{3}, \frac{1}{4}$, and $\frac{1}{5}$ are considered unit fractions. When a unit fraction is added to itself multiple times, the result is a larger fraction. For example, $\frac{1}{8} + \frac{1}{8} + \frac{1}{8} = \frac{3}{8}$.

The opposite of this is **decomposing** a fraction into the sum of its unit fractions.

$\frac{5}{6}$ is the result of combining $\frac{1}{6}$ five times.

$$\frac{5}{6} = \frac{1}{6} + \frac{1}{6} + \frac{1}{6} + \frac{1}{6} + \frac{1}{6}$$

Decomposing Fractions

When a fraction is decomposed, it is **split up** into **smaller** fractions. The sum of these smaller fractions is the original fraction. For example, $\frac{7}{8}$ can be split up into the sum of $\frac{1}{8}+\frac{1}{8}+\frac{1}{8}+\frac{1}{8}+\frac{1}{8}+\frac{1}{8}+\frac{1}{8}$. However, this is not the only way to decompose $\frac{7}{8}$.

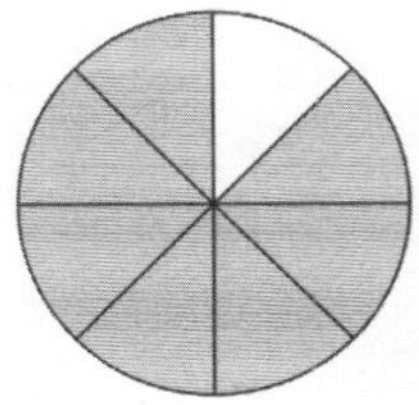

For example, the model below shows 7 shaded shares out of 8, or the fraction $\frac{7}{8}$. The fraction $\frac{7}{8}$ can be created in many ways. For example, $\frac{2}{8}+\frac{4}{8}+\frac{1}{8}$ has a sum of $\frac{7}{8}$.

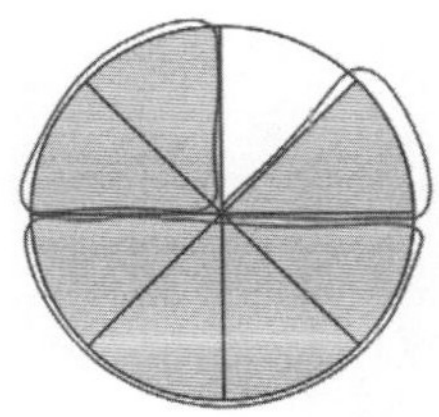

Adding and Subtracting Fractions with Like Denominators

When adding or subtracting fractions, it is important to make sure that the denominators are the same. If the fractions have like denominators, add the numerators together and leave the denominator the same. Consider the diagram below. Each whole is divided into 8 equal shares. The circle on the left shows 2 out of 8, or $\frac{2}{8}$. The circle on the right shows 6 out of 8, or $\frac{6}{8}$.

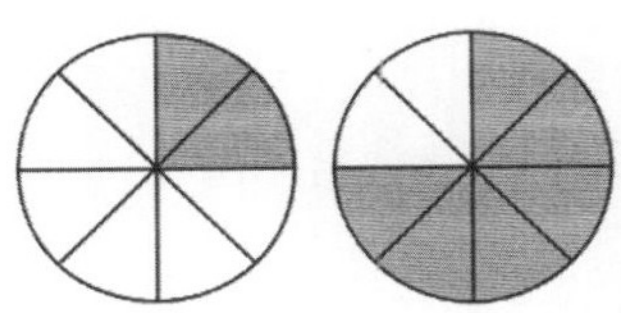

Both fractions have the same denominators so their numerators can be combined. $\frac{2}{8}+\frac{6}{8}$ combines to $\frac{8}{8}$. Another way to express $\frac{8}{8}$ is 1 whole.

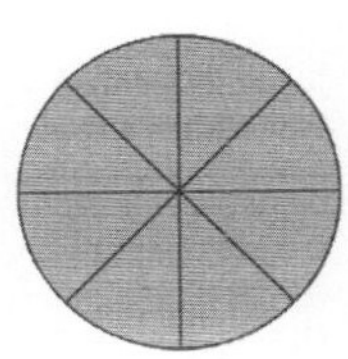

A picture or model is a great way to represent addition and subtraction of fractions. However, there is a shortcut! When denominators are the same, simply add or subtract the numerators.

$$\frac{2}{7}+\frac{4}{7}=\frac{6}{7}$$

Notice how the denominator, 7, stays the same and the numerators are added.

$$\frac{8}{9} - \frac{3}{9} = \frac{5}{9}$$

Notice how the denominator, 9, stays the same and the numerators are subtracted.

EXAMPLE

Write and solve an addition equation that represents adding the top fraction to the bottom fraction illustrated below.

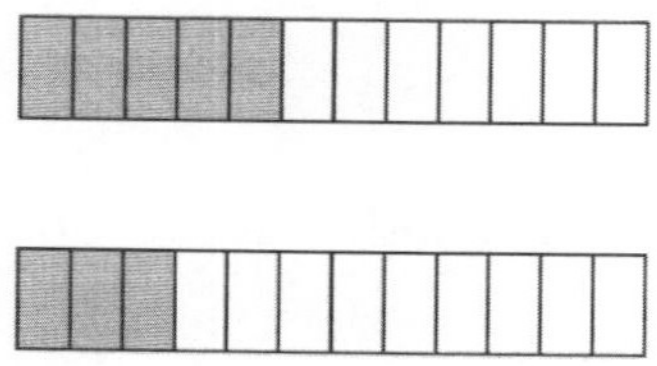

Top fraction: $\frac{5}{12}$

Bottom fraction: $\frac{3}{12}$

Both fractions have the same denominator, so they can be combined.

$$\frac{5}{12} + \frac{3}{12} = \frac{8}{12}$$

$\frac{8}{12}$ can be simplified by dividing the numerator and denominator by 4. $\frac{8}{12}$ becomes $\frac{2}{3}$.

$$\frac{5}{12} + \frac{3}{12} = \frac{8}{12} = \frac{2}{3}$$

EXAMPLE

Model the subtraction equation on the number line, then solve: $\frac{6}{10} - \frac{2}{10} = ?$

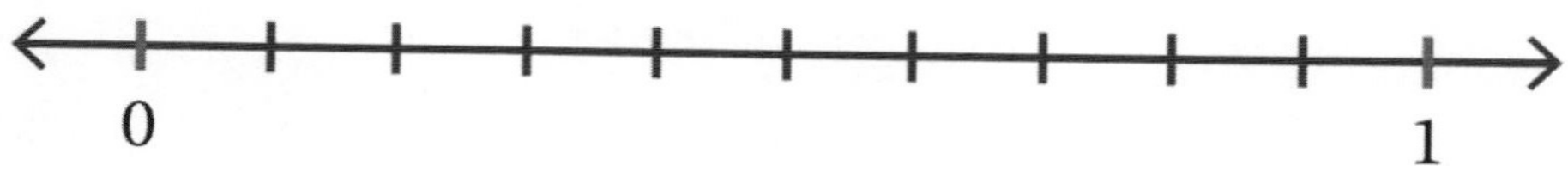

The number line is divided into 10 equal shares. Each hash mark represents $\frac{1}{10}$.

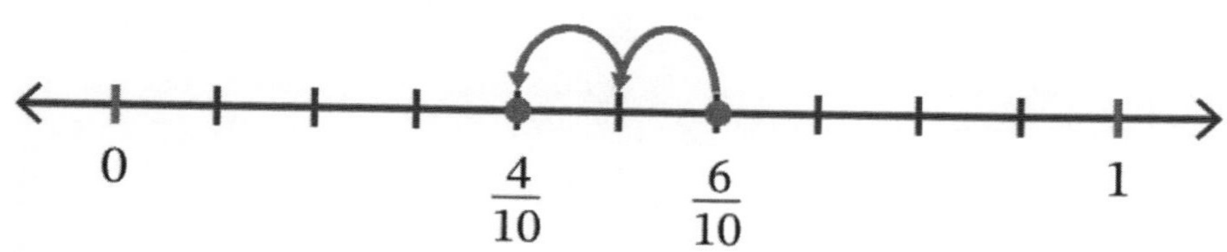

The red dot starts at $\frac{6}{10}$. The arrows show 2 jumps back, which represents subtraction of $\frac{2}{10}$: $\frac{6}{10} - \frac{2}{10} = \frac{4}{10}$.

Representing Real-World Relationships

Input-output tables are used to show the relationship between two variables. For example, consider the muffin pan below.

Each pan can hold 15 muffins. This means that 15 muffins can be baked in 1 pan, 30 muffins can be baked in 2 pans, 45 muffins can be baked in 3 pans, and so on. These values can be placed in an input-output table to show the relationship between the number of pans and the total number of muffins.

Pans	1	2	3	4
Muffins	15	30	45	60

The rule for this input-output table is number of muffins = number of pans × 15.

Here are some more examples:

Rule: Find y by adding 2 to x.

x	y
8	10
4	6
2	4
6	8
3	5

Rule: Find y by multiplying x by 4.

x	9	4	5	2
y	36	16	20	8

EXAMPLE

Complete the table so that the rule applies. Rule: James earns $42 per hour

Hours	1	2	3	4	5	6	7
Dollars		84				252	

The rule states that $42 is earned each hour. The number of dollars can be determined by multiplying the number of hours by 42, or by adding 42 to the previous dollar amount.

$$1 \times 42 = 42$$

$$2 \times 42 = 84$$

$$3 \times 42 = 126$$

$$4 \times 42 = 168$$

$$5 \times 42 = 210$$

$$6 \times 42 = 252$$

$$7 \times 42 = 294$$

Hours	1	2	3	4	5	6	7
Dollars	42	84	126	168	210	252	294

EXAMPLE

Write a rule that describes the relationship in the table.

x	4	5	6	7
y	32	40	48	56

Each value of y is 8 times as large as the corresponding x-value: $y = 8 \times x$. This can be expressed as "y is 8 times the value of x" or "multiply x by 8 to determine the value of y."

Measurement and Geometry

Coins and Bills

The value of a collection of coins and bills can be found by adding the values according to place value.

Place Value

	Penny	$0.01 or 1¢
	Nickel	$0.05 or 5¢
	Dime	$0.10 or 10¢
	Quarter	$0.25 or 25¢
	1-dollar bill	$1.00
	5-dollar bill	$5.00
	10-dollar bill	$10.00
	20-dollar bill	$20.00

Adding Coins and Bills

When adding coins and bills, make sure to line up the decimals.

Example

Allison has one $1-dollar bill, two quarters, and 4 dimes in her bank. Find the total amount of money in Allison's bank.

It may help to draw a picture. Write the value of each bill or coin in its picture. Then add up the bills and coins to find the total money.

$1 + 0.25 + 0.25 + 0.10 + 0.10 + 0.10 + 0.10 = 1.90$

There is $1.90 in Allison's bank.

EXAMPLE

Start by combining the bills.

$5 + 1 + 1 + 1 = 8$. So far, there are $8.

Now add the coins. There are 2 quarters, 1 nickel, and 2 dimes.

Be sure to line up the decimals when adding.

$0.25 + 0.25 + 0.1 + 0.1 + 0.05 = 0.75$, or 75 cents.

$$\begin{array}{r} 0.25 \\ 0.25 \\ 0.10 \\ 0.10 \\ +\,0.05 \\ \hline 0.75 \end{array}$$

Combine the bills and the coins: $8 + 0.75 = 8.75$, or $8.75.

$$\begin{array}{r} 8.00 \\ +\,0.75 \\ \hline 8.75 \end{array}$$

Remember, when the sum of a collection of coins exceeds 99 cents, the amount can be expressed using bills. For example, 99 pennies is 99 cents, or $0.99, but 100 pennies is 100 cents, or 1 dollar bill.

COMPARING VALUES

EXAMPLE

Compare the two sets of coins. Which set has a greater value?

Set A:

Set B:

Set A has a value of $0.70. Set B has a value of $0.55. Therefore, the value of Set A is greater than the value of Set B.

MAKING CHANGE

When making change, subtract the amount paid from the amount given. For example, if Dan gave the cashier a $5 for items that produced a total cost of $2.88, the cashier would need to give Dan his change in return. To calculate the amount needed to return to Dan, the cashier would subtract $2.88 from $5.00. This represents the equation 5.00 - 2.88 = 2.12. Therefore, Dan will receive $2.12 in change after paying for his items.

MEASUREMENT SYSTEMS

The **metric system** is a system of measurement used for identifying mass, volume, and length. Most countries in the world use the metric system when making calculations in math and science. However, the United States has another measurement system called the **customary system**. The customary system also measures mass, volume, and length, but it uses different units.

For example, the metric system has base units of meters, liters, and grams. Meters measure length, liters measure volume, and grams measure mass. The metric system is convenient in math and science because it follows the base-ten number system. This means that quick calculations and conversions can be done simply by multiplying or dividing by a power of ten. For example, 10 millimeters is equivalent to 1 centimeter.

The customary system has much more than three units. For example, when measuring volume, options include ounces, cups, pints, quarts, and gallons. Converting between units is more challenging because each unit has a different conversion factor. For example, there are 4 quarts in a gallon, but 16 ounces in a pint. Distance is measured in inches, feet, yards, and miles. Mass is similar to weight, and is measured in ounces, pounds, and tons. It is important to become familiar with units in the metric and customary systems.

LENGTH OF A SEGMENT

Length can be measured by the following customary units: inches, feet, yards, miles.

- **1 inch**: about the width of a quarter
- **1 foot**: about the height of a 2 liter soda bottle (12 inches)
- **1 yard**: about the width of a door (3 feet)
- **1 mile**: about 4 laps on an outdoor running track

Length can also be measured with metric units. The base unit for length in the metric system is meters, but other measurements for length include: kilometer, hectometer, decameter, decimeter, centimeter, millimeter.

- **1 meter:** about the width of a standard door frame

EXAMPLE

Find the length of the line segment using the ruler below. The ruler is in inches.

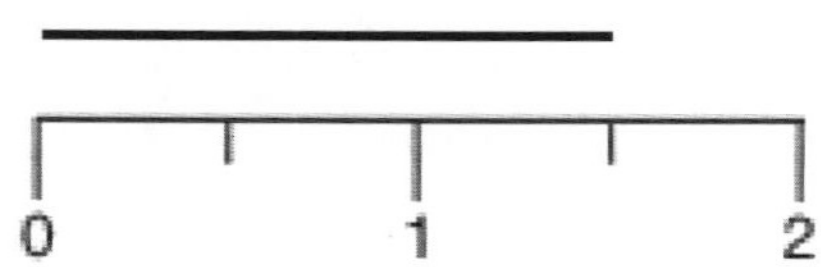

The line segment begins at 0, and ends at the mark that is halfway between 1 and 2 inches. Halfway between 1 and 2 inches is $1\frac{1}{2}$ inches. The line segment is $1\frac{1}{2}$ inches long.

VOLUME AND WEIGHT

Volume is the amount of space something fills. **Weight** is the heaviness of an object. The terms are similar, but not interchangeable. Volume is not the same as weight.

For example, consider the image below. The two spheres have the same volume because they take up the same amount of space. However, their weights are very different. One sphere weighs 12 pounds and the other weighs 1 pound. Remember, volume and weight do not describe the same thing. They are similar, but one describes how much space is filled by an object, and one describes the heaviness of an object.

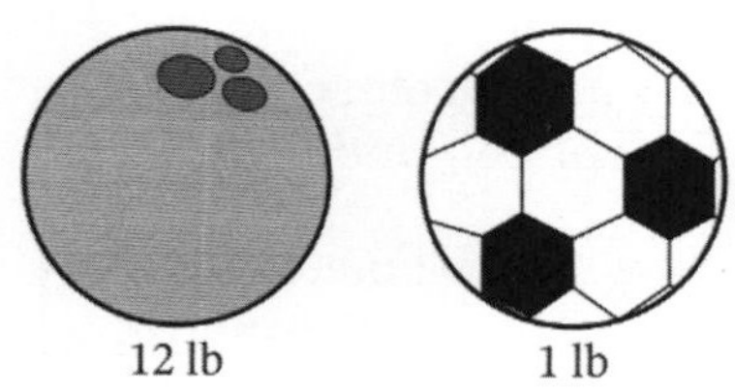

When determining how much space is filled, use volume. When determining the heaviness of an object, use weight.

Measuring Volume and Weight

Volume and weight are similar measurements but are not interchangeable. Volume measures capacity, or how much space is filled. Weight measures how heavy an object is.

Volume can be measured by the following customary units: ounces, cups, pints, quarts, gallons.

- **1 ounce**: the amount of liquid in two tablespoons
- **1 cup**: the amount of liquid in a coffee cup (8 ounces)
- **1 pint**: the amount of liquid in a small water bottle (16 ounces)
- **1 quart**: the amount of liquid in a jug of juice (2 pints)
- **1 gallon**: the amount of liquid in a large container of milk

Volume can also be measured with metric units. The base unit for volume in the metric system is liters, but other measurements for volume include: kiloliter, hectoliter, decaliter, deciliter, centiliter, milliliter.

- **1 liter:** about the volume of a large water bottle

Volume describes **capacity**. Capacity can be determined using tools such as a **beaker**. The amount of liquid in the beaker is 125 mL. This represents the volume.

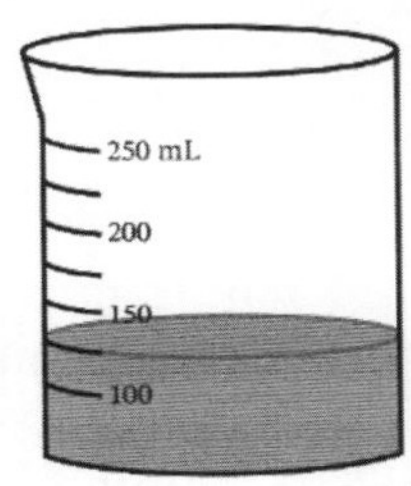

Weight can be measured by the following customary units: ounces, pounds, tons.

- **1 ounce**: about the weight of a candy bar
- **1 pound**: about the weight of a football
- **1 ton**: about the weight of a car

Weight can also be measured with metric units. The base unit for weight in the metric system is grams, but other measurements for weight include: kilogram, hectogram, decagram, decigram, centigram, milligram.

- **1 gram:** about the mass of a paperclip

Weight describes how **heavy** an object is. A **scale** can be used to determine weight. Weight is measured in ounces, pounds, or tons.

Classifying and Sorting Figures

Two-Dimensional Figures

Two-dimensional shapes can be classified by the number of sides they have. Polygons are considered **regular polygons** if all the sides are the same length. For example, a regular pentagon has 5 sides, and all of the sides are the same length. Side lengths that are the same are considered **congruent**. For example, a square has 4 congruent side lengths.

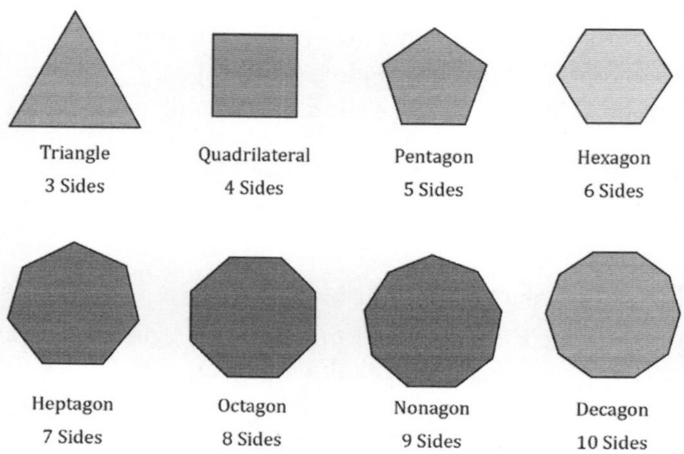

Quadrilaterals

A **quadrilateral** is a 4-sided shape. There are many subcategories of quadrilaterals. The most common are parallelogram, rhombus, rectangle, square, and trapezoid.

Parallelogram: A parallelogram has two pairs of parallel sides. It sometimes looks like a leaning rectangle.

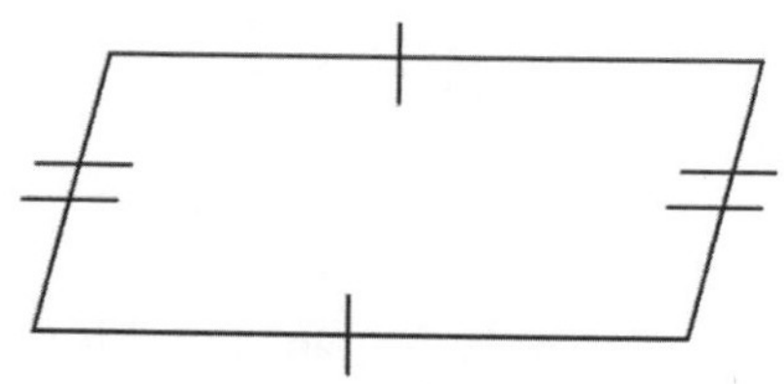

Rhombus: A rhombus is a parallelogram with four equal sides. It has no 90° angles.

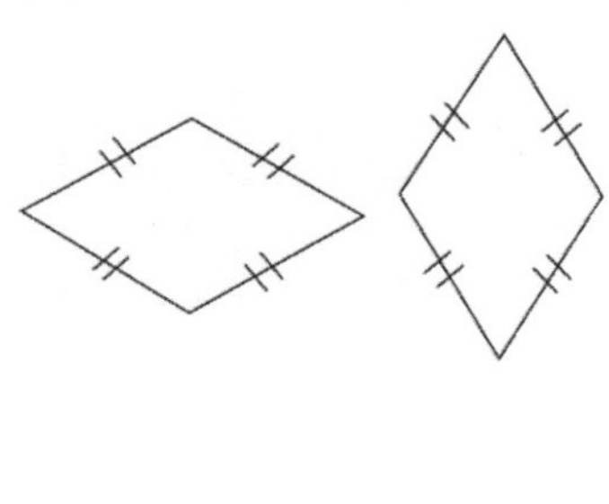

Rectangle: A rectangle has two equal parallel long sides, two equal parallel short sides, and four 90° angles.

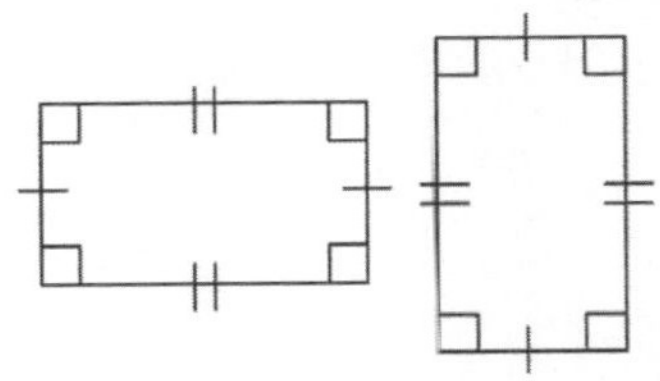

Square: A square has four equal sides. Its opposite sides are parallel, and it has four 90° angles.

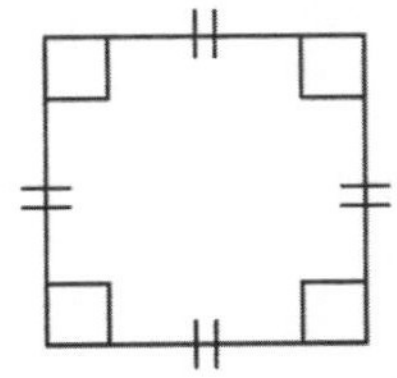

Trapezoid: A trapezoid has one pair of parallel sides and one pair of non-parallel sides.

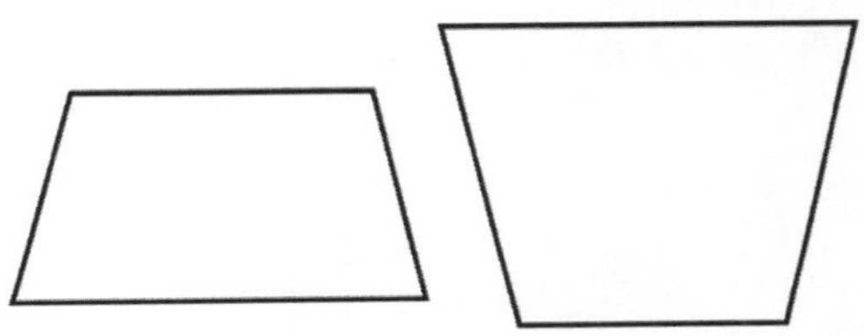

Not all 4-sided shapes fall into these categories. For example, the shapes below are quadrilaterals, but they do not fall into any of the subcategories mentioned above. They are simply referred to as quadrilaterals.

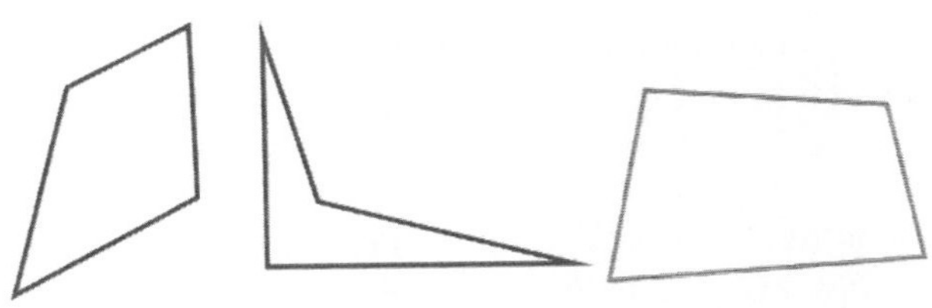

EXAMPLE

All the shapes below can be classified as ________. The top two shapes can also be classified as ________ or as ________.

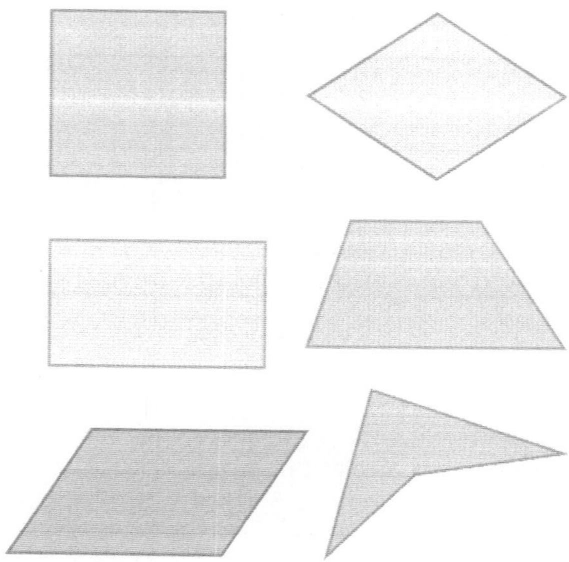

Quadrilateral: 4-sided polygon
Parallelogram: A quadrilateral that has 2 pairs of parallel sides
Rhombus: A parallelogram with 4 congruent side lengths

All the shapes below can be classified as quadrilaterals. The green and yellow shapes can also be classified as rhombi or as parallelograms.

PERIMETER

Perimeter is the distance around the outside of a two-dimensional shape. Perimeter can be calculated by finding the **sum** of a shape's **side lengths**. When a shape has **congruent** side lengths, all the sides are the same length. These shapes are called **regular polygons**.

The shape below has 6 congruent side lengths. Find the sum of the side lengths to calculate the perimeter of the regular hexagon. One side length is labeled 3 inches, therefore all of the side lengths are 3 inches. Perimeter = 3 + 3 + 3 + 3 + 3 + 3, which simplifies to $P = 18$. The perimeter of the regular hexagon is 18 inches.

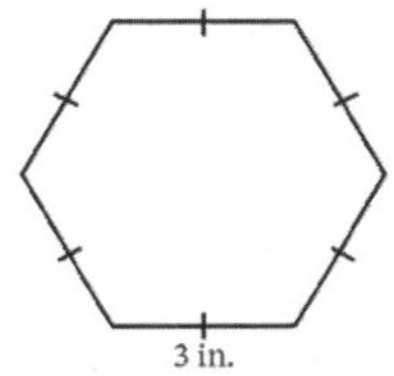

The same rules apply for polygons with missing side lengths. The triangle below has 3 congruent side lengths, and the perimeter is 18 cm. Ask the question, "__ + __ + __ = 18?" Since 6 + 6 + 6 = 18, the side lengths are all 6 cm.

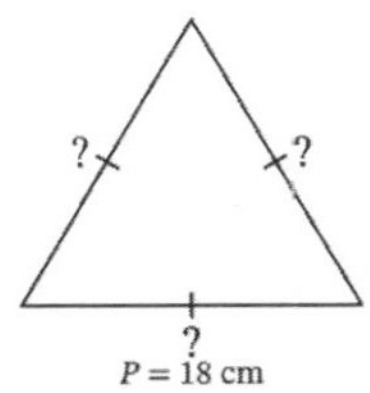

EXAMPLE

A rectangle has a length of 3 inches and a width of 1 inch. Find the perimeter of the rectangle.

Using a ruler, draw a model of the rectangle with the given side lengths.

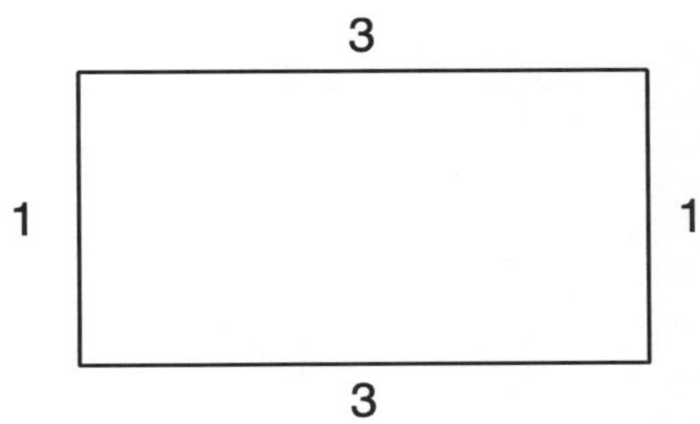

The perimeter of a rectangle is the sum of side lengths: perimeter = 3 inches + 1 inch + 3 inches + 1 inch = 8 inches.

EXAMPLE

A triangle has sides that are 6 cm, 8 cm, and 11 cm long. Find the perimeter of the triangle.

Using a ruler, draw a model of the triangle with the given side lengths.

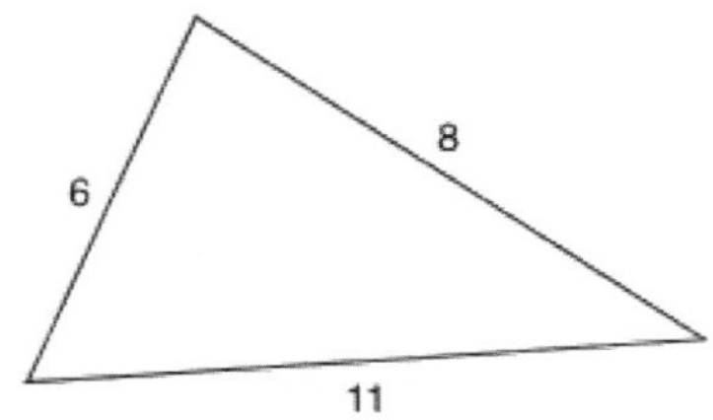

The perimeter is the sum of the side lengths: 6 cm + 8 cm + 11 cm = 25 cm.

EXAMPLE

A carpenter is building an octagonal window for a boat. The outer octagon has side lengths of 8 inches, and the inner octagon has side lengths of 7 inches. What is the difference in the perimeters of the two octagons?

Perimeter of the outer octagon: $8 + 8 + 8 + 8 + 8 + 8 + 8 + 8 = 64$. Therefore, the perimeter is 64 inches.

Perimeter of the inner octagon: $7 + 7 + 7 + 7 + 7 + 7 + 7 + 7 = 56$. Therefore, the perimeter is 56 inches.

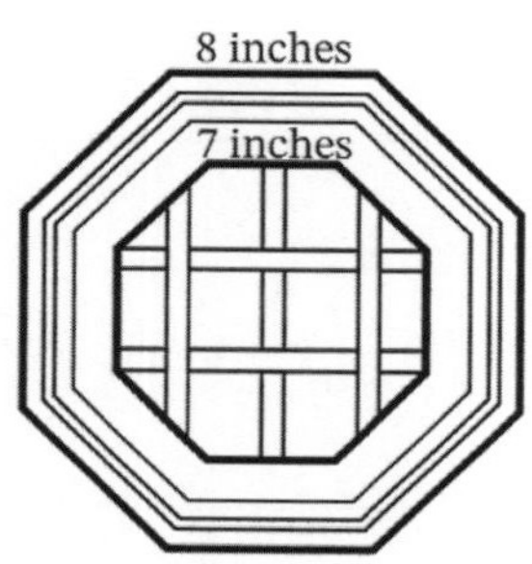

$64 - 56 = 8$, so the difference between the two perimeters is 8 inches.

AREA

AREA OF A RECTANGLE

The **area formula** for a **rectangle** is Area = Length × Width. This means the area can be determined by multiplying the number of **rows** by the number of **columns**. Think about the area of a rectangle as an array. For example, a rectangle that is 6 ft by 4 ft is essentially 6 columns and 4 rows. 6 groups of 4 is the same thing as 4 groups of 6, so the area can be calculated as 6×4 or 4×6. $6 \times 4 = 24$ and $4 \times 6 = 24$. The area is 24 square units.

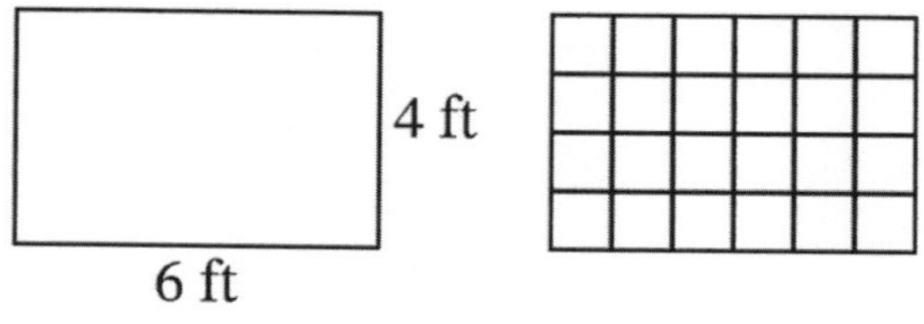

EXAMPLE

Draw a rectangle that is 8 units high and 10 units wide.

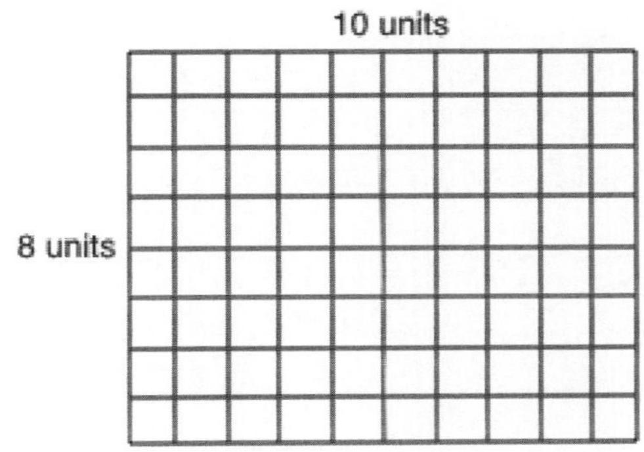

To find the area, count the squares inside the area of the rectangle. There are 80 squares; the area of the rectangle is 80 $units^2$.

EXAMPLE

Draw a square that is 7 units wide and 7 units high. Here, each circle represents one unit.

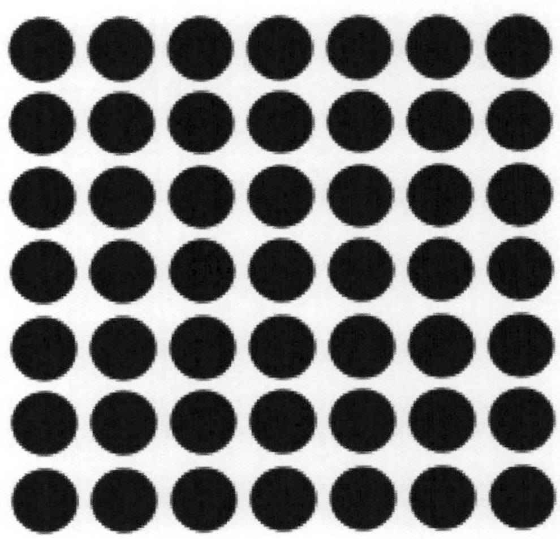

The total number of circles is the area. There are 49 circles, so the area of the square is 49 $units^2$.

EXAMPLE

A pan of fudge needs to be cut into equally sized pieces. One row is already divided. How many pieces of fudge will there be in the entire pan?

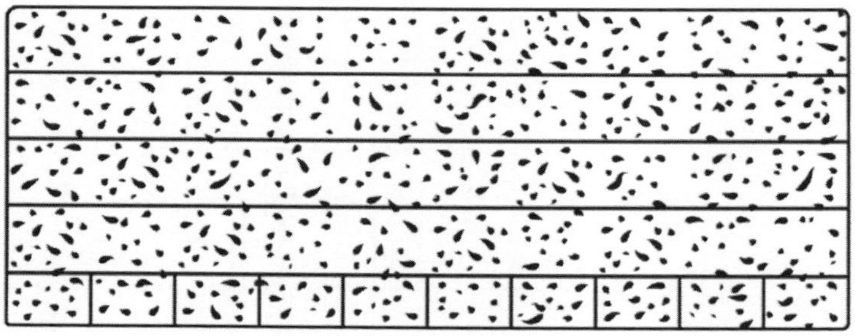

The total number of pieces can be calculated by multiplying the number of pieces in one row, by the total number of rows. This can be thought of as an array of 5 rows with 10 columns. 5 groups of 10 equals 50. The entire pan holds 50 pieces of fudge.

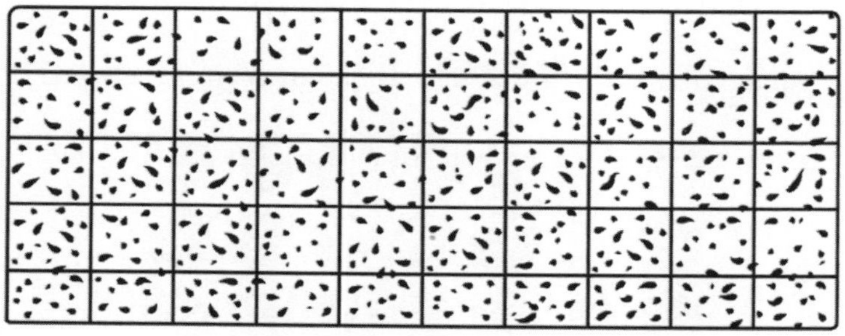

EXAMPLE

A rectangle has an area of 16 unit squares. The rectangle has two columns. How many rows does the rectangle have?

The area of the rectangle is 16 unit squares. The rectangle has 2 columns, so it must have 8 rows: $2 \times 8 = 16$. The rectangle forms an array of 2 columns and 8 rows.

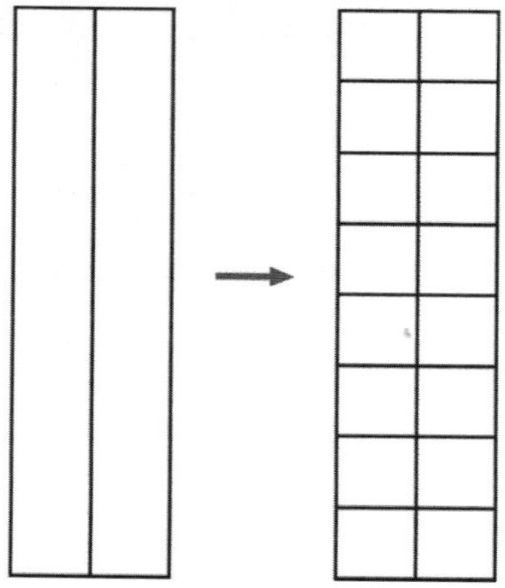

EQUAL PARTS AND AREA

There is more than one correct way to decompose, or divide, a two-dimensional figure. For example, if a pan of brownies needs to be sliced into 8 equal pieces, there are a few ways to achieve this. Consider the rectangular brownie pans below. Notice how both pans have 8 **equally sized** brownies, even though the identical pieces are not the same shape for both pans. Each brownie can be represented as the unit fraction $\frac{1}{8}$. Remember, a unit fraction has a numerator of 1.

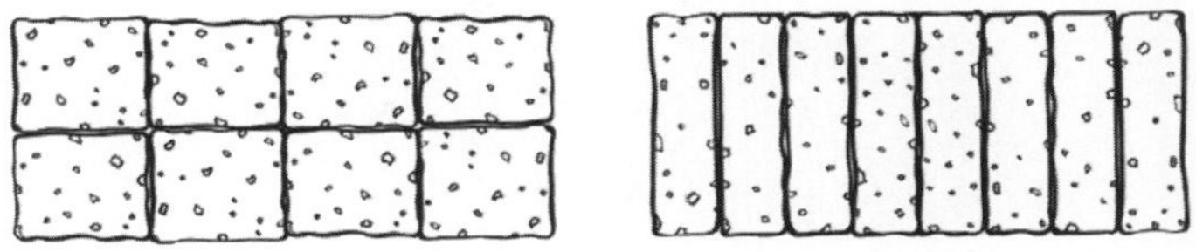

CONGRUENCY

Congruent figures are the same size and shape. This means that all of the sides are the same length, and all of the angles are the same measure. The two rectangles below are congruent.

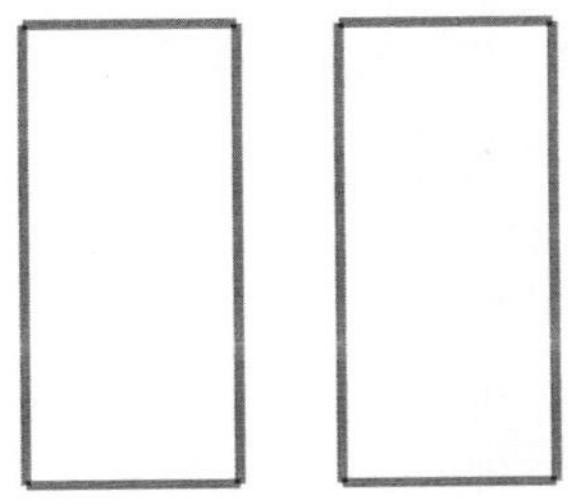

CONGRUENT PARTS OF A SQUARE

The congruent parts are the parts of the square that are the same size. On a square, all side lengths are equal and all angles are equal. The congruent parts are the side and angles. For example:

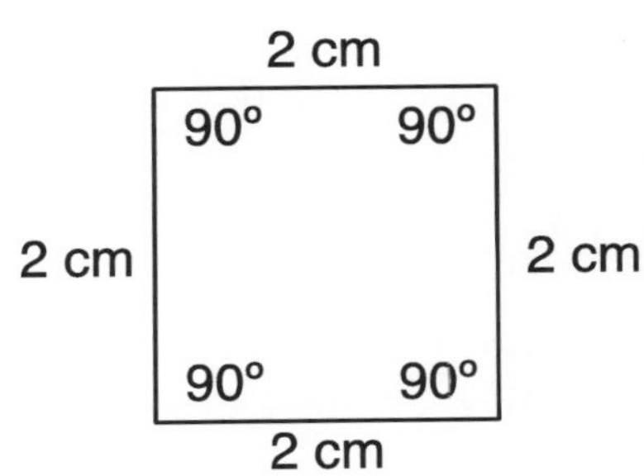

CONGRUENT PARTS OF A PARALLELOGRAM

A parallelogram is a quadrilateral where pairs of opposite sides are parallel. Opposite sides of a parallelogram are congruent, and opposite angles are also congruent. For example:

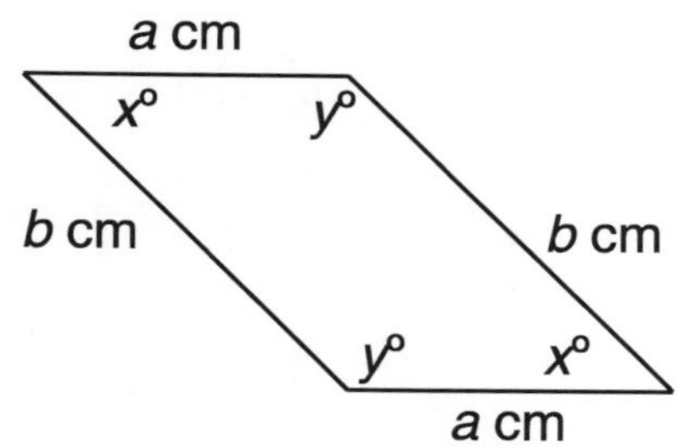

CONGRUENT TRIANGLE

EXAMPLE

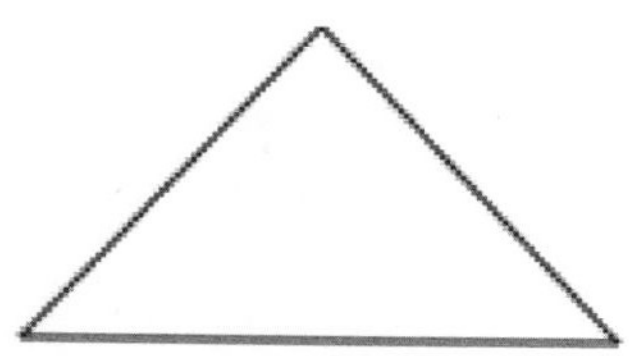

A congruent triangle can be made by moving the original triangle left, right, up, or down. The congruent figure below, with the dashed lines, was moved up and to the right.

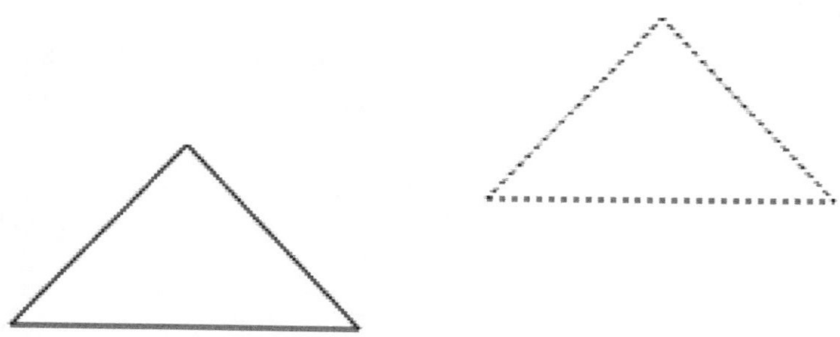

EXAMPLE

Create a congruent triangle to the one below by turning the triangle.

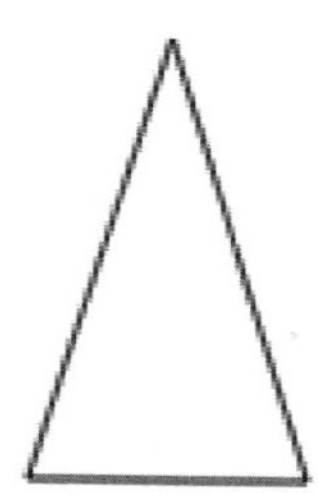

To create a congruent triangle by rotating, first draw a point of rotation. The point can be outside, inside, or on the figure. Then pick a number of degrees to rotate the figure. For example, rotate the figure 90º.

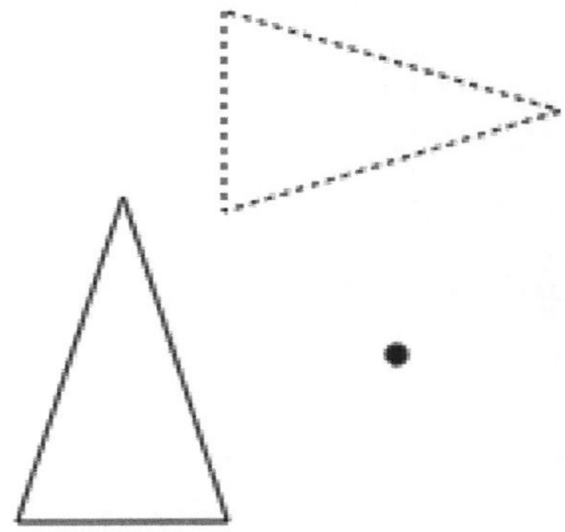

Points, Lines, Rays, and Angles

A **point** is an exact location with no size. This often appears as a dot, and is usually labeled with a letter, such as Point A.

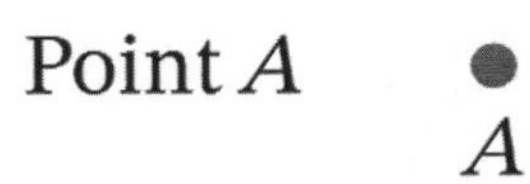

A **line** is a straight path that extends in opposite directions. A line does not have a width, and it extends indefinitely in both directions. Lines are labeled with letters representing points on the line, such as $\overleftrightarrow{AB}$.

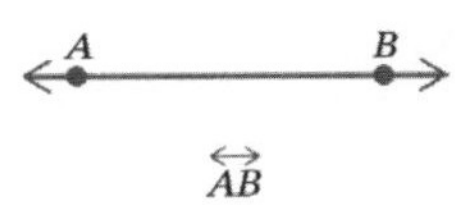

A **line segment** is a part of a line. A line segment has endpoints, beginning and ending at a point labeled with a letter, such as $\overline{AB}$.

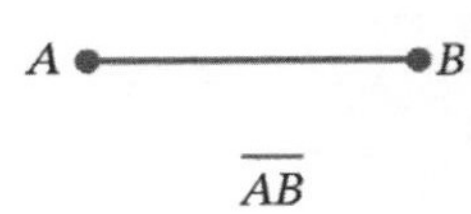

A **ray** is a part of a line that starts at an endpoint and then extends out indefinitely. Rays are labeled starting with a letter at the endpoint and ending with a letter representing another point on the ray, such as $\overrightarrow{AB}$.

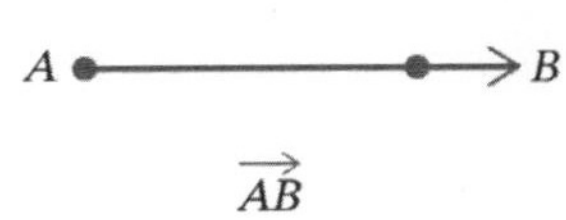

An **angle** is formed when two straight lines or rays meet at a common endpoint. The two rays below form an angle.

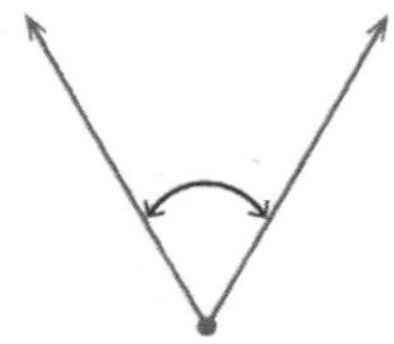

Parallel lines extend side-by-side and never intersect. To help visualize parallel lines, think of train tracks.

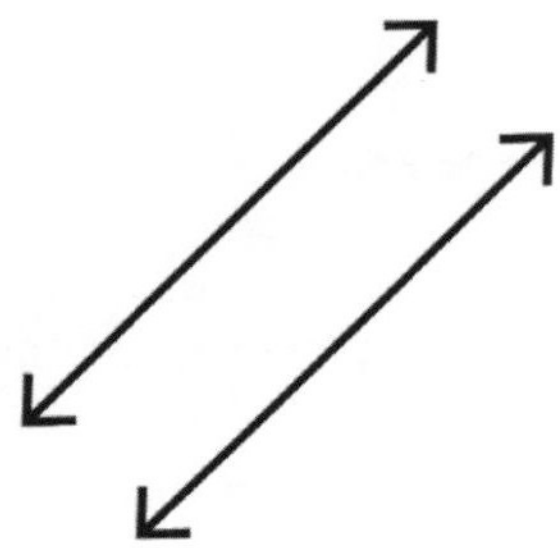

Perpendicular lines intersect to form a right angle. To help visualize perpendicular lines, think of a corner or a T-shape.

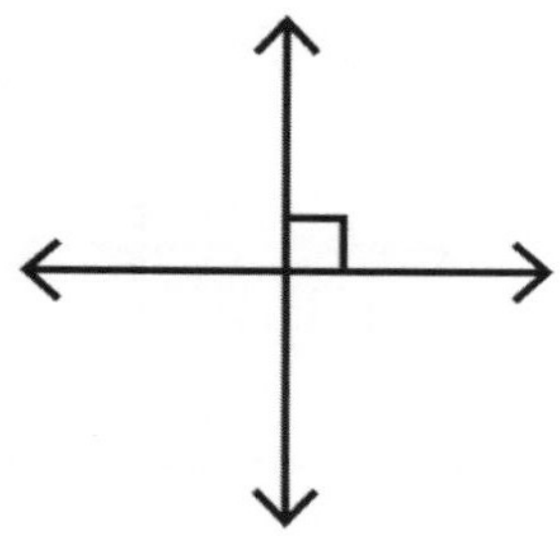

Review Video: Parallel and Perpendicular Lines
Visit mometrix.com/academy and enter code: 815923

TIME

Draw the time 7:20 on an analog clock and a digital clock.

On the analog clock, the small hand will be just after the 7, showing it is just after 7 o'clock. The big hand will be at 20 minutes, which is at 4.

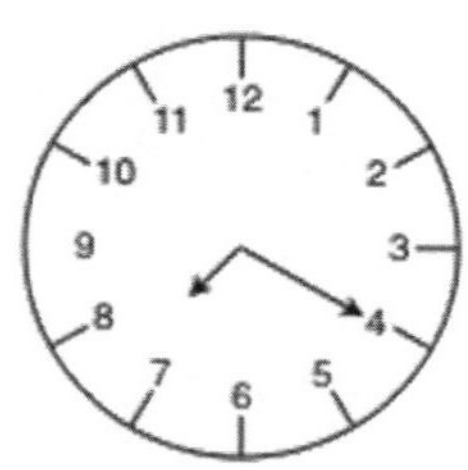

On a digital clock, the time will be written in the order: hours, then minutes. Since the hour is only one digit, there may be a 0 before the 7.

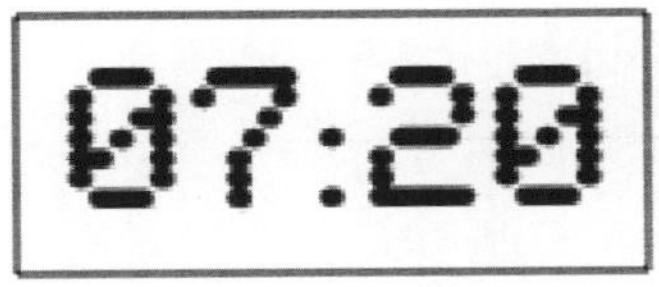

Find the time on the clock below.

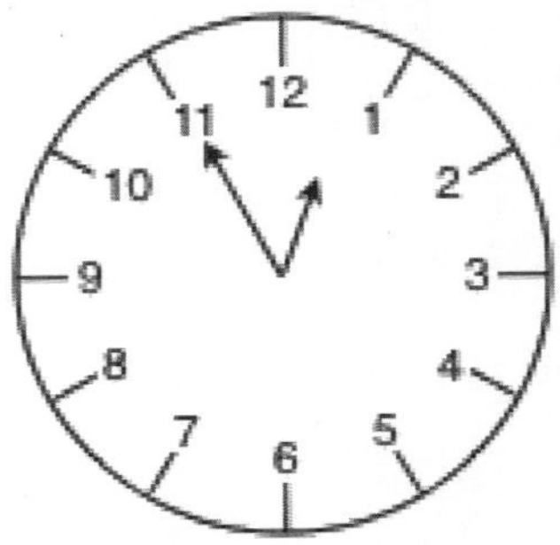

The big hand is on the 11, so the minutes is 55. The small hand is just before the 1, which means that it is close to 1 o'clock, but it is not yet 1 o'clock. It is still 12 o'clock. The time is 12:55.

Time Intervals

Things to remember:

There are 60 seconds in 1 minute.

There are 60 minutes in 1 hour.

There are 24 hours in 1 day.

There are 365 days in 1 year.

Adding and Subtracting Time

When adding or subtracting time in minutes, an hour can be visualized as 4 sections of 15 minutes.

$\frac{1}{4}$ of an hour: 15 minutes

$\frac{2}{4}$ of an hour: 30 minutes

$\frac{3}{4}$ of an hour: 45 minutes

$\frac{4}{4}$ of an hour: 60 minutes

STRATEGIES FOR ADDING AND SUBTRACTING TIME

For example, if a student practices the piano for 15 minutes a day, for 4 days, how long have they practiced in all?

Use a model. Each 15-minute session represents $\frac{1}{4}$ of an hour. $15 + 15 + 15 + 15 = 60$. So, the student has practiced for 60 minutes, which is 1 hour.

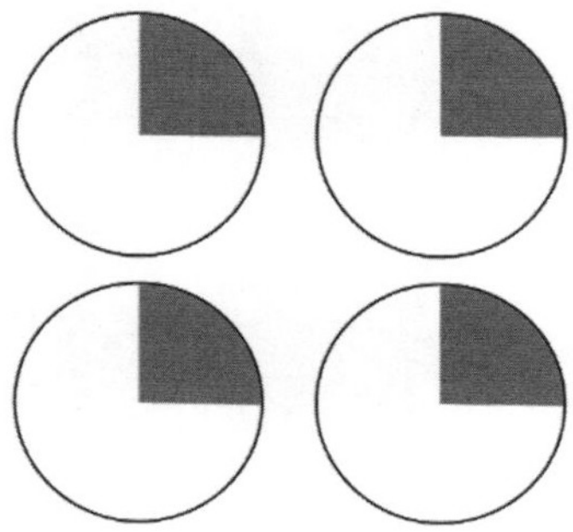

Using sections of the clock to add or subtract is a great way to solve problems mentally. Remember, one quarter of an hour is 15 minutes, and one half of an hour is 30 minutes. Skip counting by 15 or 30 is an efficient way to solve problems involving elapsed time. This also works for subtraction problems.

Consider the following scenario: A student studied 45 minutes for a math test, and 15 minutes for a science test. How much longer did the student study for the math test than the science test?

Math: 45 minutes

Science: 15 minutes

Subtract the time between studying for math and studying for science: $45 - 15 = 30$. This represents half an hour. The student spent 30 minutes more studying for the math test than the science test.

TEMPERATURE

Find the temperature, in degrees Fahrenheit, on the thermometer below:

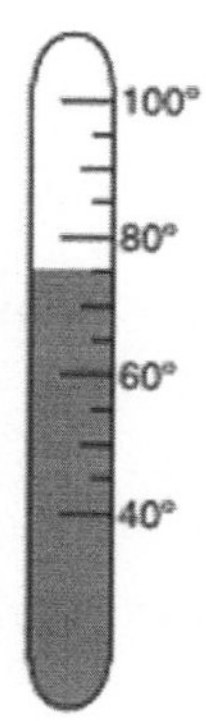

The temperature on the thermometer is halfway between 70º and 80º. The temperature halfway between 70º and 80º is 75º F.

Probability, Statistics, Patterns, Functions, and Algebra

Probability

Probability is the likelihood of a certain outcome occurring for a given event. An **event** is any situation that produces a result. It could be something as simple as flipping a coin or as complex as launching a rocket. Simple probability can be found using the formula below.

$$P = \frac{\text{Number of desired outcomes}}{\text{Number of total possible outcomes}}$$

Example

Darla is going to make 24 cookies total. 5 of them will be chocolate chip, 15 of them will be sugar, and 4 of them will be snickerdoodles. If she randomly selected a cookie off the trays, what would be the likelihood that she selects a sugar cookie?

Since 15 out of the 24 total cookies are sugar cookies, the probability is $\frac{15}{24}$ which simplifies to $\frac{5}{8}$. The likelihood that she selects a sugar cookie is very high since majority of her cookies on the trays are sugar cookies.

Summarizing Data

Data refers to a collection of information. For example, when a survey is conducted, data points are collected. It is helpful to organize these data points before displaying the information in a table or graph. Typical data displays include bar graphs, frequency tables, pictographs, and dot plots.

Bar Graphs

Bar graphs use horizontal or vertical bars to represent the total amount for each category. For example, this bar graph shows the number of votes for a variety of snacks. The length of the bar represents the number of votes. Notice how the red popcorn bar represents 5 votes, the green crackers bar represents 2 votes, and so on. The interval should always be scaled and consistent when displaying data graphically. For example, the number of votes on this bar graph increases by 2 consistently.

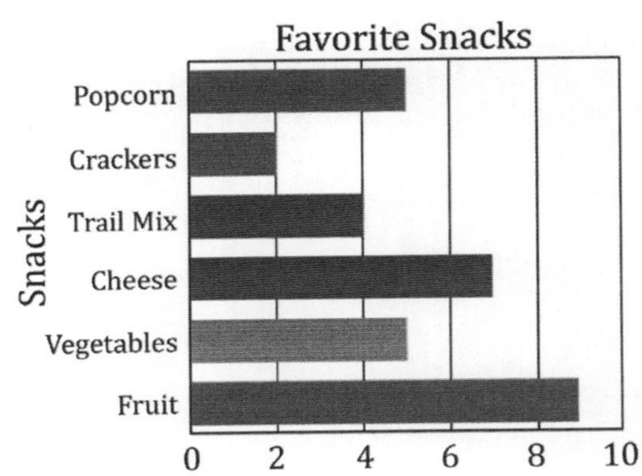

Frequency Tables

Frequency tables are used to show how often, or frequently, an event or value occurs. Frequency tables often use tally marks to show the total frequency for each category.

Favorite Club

Club	Tally	Frequency
Hockey	卌 |||	8
Badminton	卌 ||	7
Football	卌	5

Pictographs

Data can be summarized by studying graphical displays such as these. Consider the pictograph below. The **pictograph** uses pictures to represent the value for each category. In this pictograph, each picture represents 1 student. The pictograph shows the variety of ways students in a 3rd grade class commute to school each day. The graph can be used to summarize the data that was collected. For example, since each picture represents 1 student, we know there are 20 students in the class. We also know the most common mode of transportation is taking the bus, and the least common mode of transportation is walking on foot.

Ways to Get to School

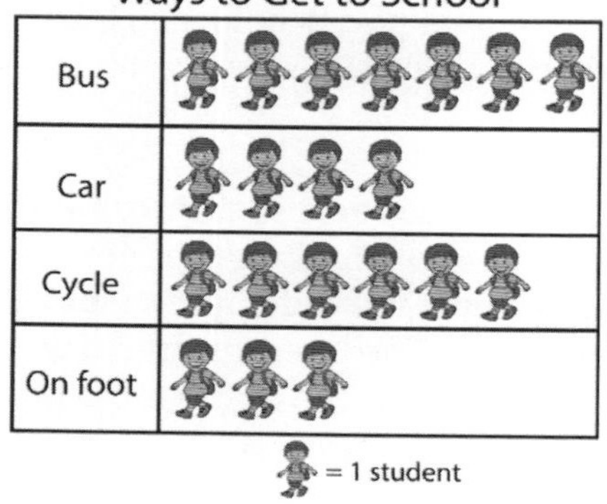

Review Video: Pictographs
Visit mometrix.com/academy and enter code: 147860

EXAMPLE

Based on the information in the bar graph, how many more students prefer math or science than social studies or ELA?

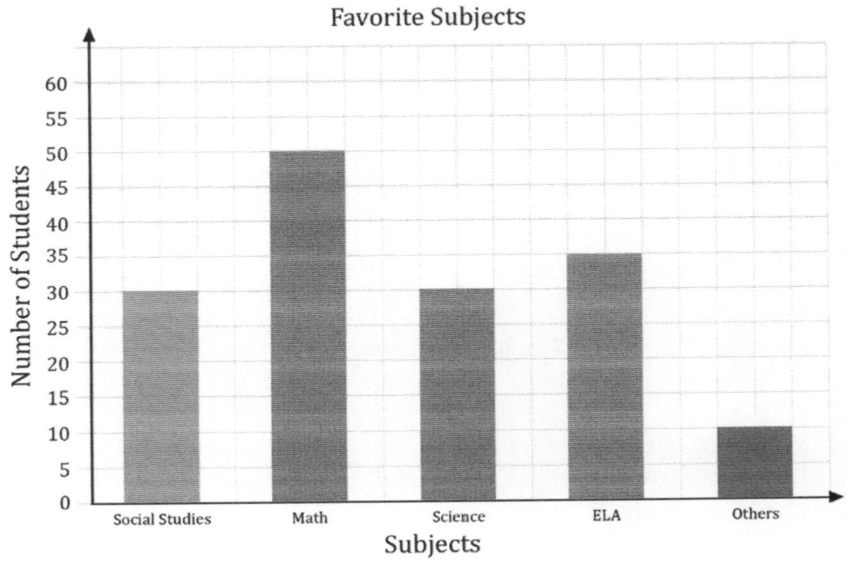

Students that prefer math or science: $50 + 30 = 80$.
Students that prefer social studies or ELA: $30 + 35 = 65$.
The difference: $80 - 65 = 15$.
There are 15 more students who prefer math or science than social studies or ELA.

EXAMPLE

Which day of the week has a value of 30 cars?

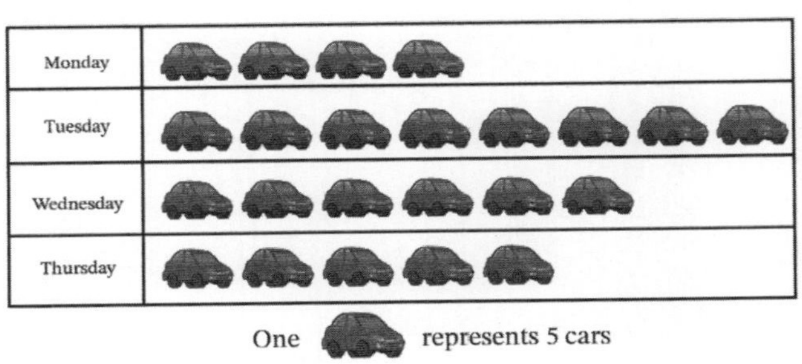

Each car in the pictograph represents 5 cars.
Monday shows 4 cars: $4 \times 5 = 20$ total cars.
Tuesday shows 8 cars: $8 \times 5 = 40$ total cars.
Wednesday shows 6 cars: $6 \times 5 = 30$ total cars.
Thursday shows 5 cars: $5 \times 5 = 25$ total cars.
Wednesday has a value of 30 total cars.

PATTERNS

A pattern is a particular arrangement of shapes, colors, pictures, numbers, objects, and other various things that repeats. Each pattern has a specific rule to follow. Patterns can also be referred to as sequences.

EXAMPLE 1

Find the next number in each pattern:

1) 2, 4, 6, 8, ...

2) 5, 10, 15, 20, ...

3) 60, 50, 40, 30, ...

1) The numbers are increasing by 2. Add 2 to the last number to find the next number: 2, 4, 6, 8, 8 + 2 = 10.

2) The numbers are increasing by 5. Add 5 to the last number to find the next number: 5, 10, 15, 20, 20 + 5 = 25.

3) The numbers are decreasing by 10. Subtract 10 from the last number to find the next number: 60, 50, 40, 30, 30 – 10 = 20.

EXAMPLE 2

Draw the next figure in this pattern:

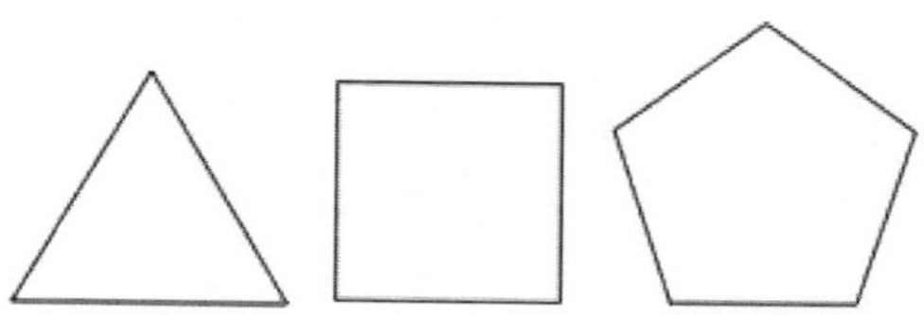

Look at the sides of each figure.

Figure 1: 3 sides

Figure 2: 4 sides

Figure 2: 5 sides

The number of sides on each figure is increasing by 1. The next figure will have 6 sides.

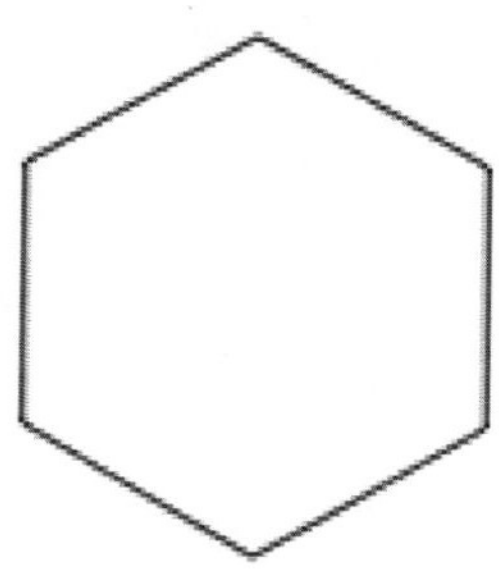

EXAMPLE 3

Find the next figure in the pattern.

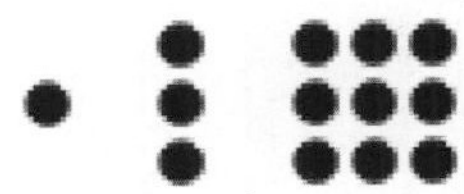

The first figure has 1 dot. The second has 3 dots. The third has 9 dots. Each figure is 3 times the size of the figure before it. The next figure will be three of the last figure:

A figure that includes three of the last figure has $3 \cdot 9 = 27$ dots.

FINDING UNKNOWN NUMBERS

INVERSE OPERATIONS

Multiplication and division go hand in hand. Division and multiplication are considered **inverse operations**, which means they are the reverse, or opposite, of each other. This can be helpful when there is an **unknown number** in an equation. For example, $4 \times ? = 24$ is a multiplication equation that can be solved using division. $24 \div 4 = 6$, therefore $4 \times 6 = 24$. The missing number is 6.

Let's try another example: $72 \div ? = 9$. This is a division equation that can be solved using multiplication. What number times 9 equals 72? The missing number is 8.

FACT FAMILIES

Don't forget to use **fact families** when solving equations with **missing numbers**.

For example, the equations $5 \times 8 = 40$, $8 \times 5 = 40$, $40 \div 5 = 8$, $40 \div 8 = 5$ represent a fact family. The same three numbers are used in all the equations. This can be helpful when one of the numbers is missing. For example, $8 \times ? = 40$. Remember the fact families. 8 groups of 5 equals 40, so the missing number is 5.

$$\text{Factor} \times \text{Factor} = \text{Product}$$

$$8 \times 5 = 40$$

8 and 5 are considered factors, and 40 is the product.

EQUIVALENT MATHEMATICAL RELATIONSHIPS

Equations can be used to represent equivalent mathematical relationships. Equations consist of two equivalent expressions joined together by an equal sign.

EXAMPLE

Write and solve a subtraction equation that matches the model below.

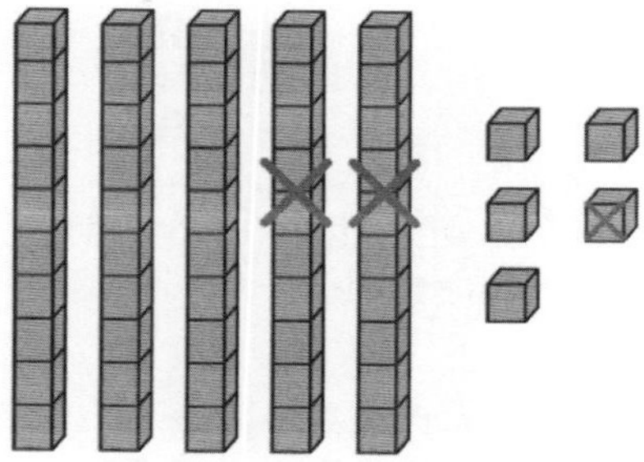

The model shows 5 groups of ten plus 5 groups of one, which represents 55. Then 2 groups of ten and 1 group of one are crossed out. This represents subtraction of 21. This leaves 3 groups of ten and 4 groups of one. So, $55 - 21$ leaves 34 remaining. The answer is $55 - 21 = 34$.

EXAMPLE

Write two multiplication equations the array below can represent.

The array shows rows and columns of stars. This can be described as 5 rows of 6, or 6 rows of 5. Both scenarios have a product of 30.

The answers are $5 \times 6 = 30$ and $6 \times 5 = 30$.

EXAMPLE

Use the numbers 3, 6, and 18 to write four equations using multiplication and division.

The numbers 3, 6, and 18 form a fact family.

3 groups of 6 equals 18: $3 \times 6 = 18$.

6 groups of 3 equals 18: $6 \times 3 = 18$.

18 divided into 3 equal groups results in 6 per group: $18 \div 3 = 6$.

18 divided into 6 equal groups results in 3 per group: $18 \div 6 = 3$.

The answers are $3 \times 6 = 18$, $6 \times 3 = 18$, $18 \div 3 = 6$, $18 \div 6 = 3$.

Reading

Word Analysis and Vocabulary

Vowels and Consonants

Vowels and consonants describe the sounds in the English language. **Vowels** are the sounds made with only the voice, such as /a/, /e/, /i/, /o/, and /u/. Sometimes the letter y can make an /i/ sound. Consonants make up all of the other sounds in English. Consonants are sounded out by using the tongue, teeth, and lips.

Syllables

Syllables are the individual sounds that make up spoken words. Syllables can be determined by saying a word out loud and listening to what the individual sounds are. Some people split sounds up differently, but the important part of syllables is knowing where each sound in a word starts and stops.

One Syllable	Two Syllable	Three Syllable	Four Syllable
Bat	Draw-ing	Ba-tter-y	Com-for-ta-ble
Car	Foot-ball	Com-put-er	In-vis-i-ble
Home	Wa-ter	Flam-in-go	Wat-er-mel-on

Sometimes, words are diagrammed using the letters v and c to describe the vowels and consonants in the word. This helps to determine what types of syllables the word contains.

	Closed Syllables	Open Syllables	VCe Syllables
Word	Cat	Banana	Ripe
Pronunciation	/Kat/	/Buh-Na-Nuh/	/Rīp/
Syllables	CVC	CV-CV-CV	CVC

Notice how in the first example, cat is one syllable, which is made up of a consonant sound from the letter c, a vowel from the letter a, and another consonant sound from the letter t. In the second example, banana is three syllables, each of which has a consonant followed by a vowel.

Closed Syllables

Closed syllables are the easiest to recognize. They are marked by a consonant sound closing off the beginning or end of a syllable.

Open Syllables

Open syllable refers to the beginning or end of a syllable that does not have a consonant closing it off. Examples of this include the words *egg* and *blue.* The number and placement of consonants in different open syllables can affect the way the vowel is pronounced in each syllable.

	VCCV	VCV
Word	Tennis, Method	Robin, Tiger
Pronunciation	/Ten-is/, /Meth-od /	/Rob-in/, /Tī-ger/
Syllables	VC/CV, VCC/V	VC/V, V/CV

VCe Syllables

VCe syllables refer to words that have a silent e in them. The letter e is included to help identify the word when reading it, but the e sound is not spoken. Examples of words with silent e sounds are *bite, cake, flute,* and *tube.*

VV Syllables

When two vowels appear next to each other in a word, they may work together to make a single sound. However, when the vowels do not make one sound together, they mark the end of one syllable and the beginning of another syllable. These are VV syllables, also called vowel teams. For example, *duel, flour,* and *diary* all contain VV syllables.

R-Controlled Vowel Syllables

R-controlled syllables are formed when an *r* comes after a vowel. In r-controlled syllables, the vowel is paired with the *r* and makes a unique sound. Examples of words with r-controlled syllables are *jar, teacher, fir, torn,* and *spur.*

Final Stable Syllables

When a word ends in a Cle syllable, or a consonant followed by *le,* it has a final stable syllable. The syllable is made of these three letters. Examples of words with final stable syllables are *spectacle, thimble,* and *giggle.*

Homophones

Homophones are words that sound the same when spoken aloud, but which have different definitions. **Homophones** are usually spelled differently. Below is a list of common homophones.

Word 1	Word 2	Word 3
Allowed	Aloud	
Ate	Eight	
Be	Bee	
Blew	Blue	
Board	Bored	
Cell	Sell	
Dear	Deer	
Eye	I	
Here	Hear	
Hour	Our	
Its	It's	
Knot	Not	

Word 1	Word 2	Word 3
Night	Knight	
Mail	Male	
Pair	Pear	Pare
Plane	Plain	
Right	Write	
Road	Rode	
Some	Sum	
Sun	Son	
There	Their	They're
Two	To	Too
Way	Weigh	
Week	Weak	
Whole	Hole	

COMMONLY MISSPELLED HOMOPHONES

TO, TOO, AND TWO

To can be an adverb or a preposition for showing direction, purpose, and relationship. A dictionary can also be used to see the many other ways to use *to* in a sentence.

Examples: I went to the store. | I want to go with you.

Too is an adverb that means *also, as well, very,* or *in excess.*

Examples: I can walk a mile too. | You have eaten too much.

Two is a number.

Example: You have two minutes left.

THERE, THEIR, AND THEY'RE

There can be an adjective, adverb, or pronoun. Often, *there* is used to show a place or to start a sentence.

Examples: I went there yesterday. | There is something in his pocket.

Their is a pronoun that is used to show ownership.

Examples: He is their father. | This is their fourth apology this week.

They're is a contraction of *they are.*

Example: Did you know that they're in town?

KNEW AND NEW

Knew is the past tense of *know.*

Example: I knew the answer.

New is an adjective that means something is current, has not been used, or is modern.

Example: This is my new phone.

Its and It's

Its is a possessive pronoun that shows ownership.

Example: The guitar is in its case.

It's is a contraction of *it is.*

Example: It's an honor and a privilege to meet you.

Your and You're

Your is a pronoun that shows ownership.

Example: This is your moment to shine.

You're is a contraction of *you are.*

Example: Yes, you're correct.

Example

In the passage below, choose the correctly spelled word from each pair in parentheses.

My grandparents gave me a (knew/new) raincoat when I visited them yesterday. It was the perfect gift because it started raining when I left (their/there) house! The rain was very heavy, but the raincoat kept me (drie/dry) and warm. When I got home, I wrote and mailed them a letter to thank them for (their/thier) useful gift.

The first set of words is *knew* and *new*. Remember that homophones are words that are spelled differently but sound the same when spoken out loud. These words have different meanings, so it is important to choose the correct homophone carefully. In this sentence, the word is being used to describe a raincoat, so it must be an adjective. *Knew* is the past tense form of the verb *know*, while *new* is an adjective. *New* is the correct choice for the first set of words.

The next set of words is *their* and *there*. This is another set of homophones! Remember what each spelling means. *There* is most commonly used to show location, and *their* is a possessive pronoun. How is the word used in the sentence? It comes before *house* and tells who the house belongs to. Since *their* is used to show ownership, it is the correct choice in this set.

The third set of words is *drie* and *dry*. One of these words is spelled correctly, while the other is not. Remember that every word must have at least one vowel, and *y* can sometimes act as a vowel. There is not always a rule for when a word should end in *ie* or *y*, so this is an example of a word that should be memorized. *Dry* is the correct spelling.

The final set of words is their and thier. Remember the rule for spelling words that use *e* and *i* together. In this set, there is no *c* and the vowels do not make a long *a* sound together. The *i* must come before the *e* in this case, so *their* is the correct choice.

Root Words, Prefixes, and Suffixes

The root, prefix, and suffix are parts of a word. The **root** is the main part of a word. It is what a **prefix** or **suffix** is attached to. A prefix goes on the front of a root word to make a new word. A suffix goes on the end of a root word to make a new word. Some words have both a prefix and a suffix. Many words have one or the other. The root, prefix, and suffix all have different meanings. By studying the parts of a word, the reader can figure out the meaning of a word.

Common Prefixes

Prefix	Meaning	Example
pre-	before	preview (to view before)
im-	not	impossible (not possible)
non-	not	nonpaid (not paid)
dis-	not	disagree (not agree)
in-	in, into, not	injustice (an action that is not just)

Common Suffixes

Suffix	Meaning	Example
-ness	state of being	darkness (being dark)
-y	characterized by	cloudy (characterized by clouds)
-ful	full of	truthful (full of truth)
-er	a person connected with	teacher (a person connected with teaching)
-able	can be done	likeable (can be liked)

Example

Figure out the meaning of the word *unhappy* by using knowledge of words parts.

In the word *unhappy*, the root word *happy* means "pleased with." For instance, a student might be happy with his or her test score. The prefix *un-* means "not." The word *unhappy* means "not pleased." A student might be unhappy with a test score, too.

Example

Figure out the meaning of *harmful* from its word parts.

Harmful is made up of a root and a suffix. The root is *harm.* The word *harm* means "to hurt." The suffix is *-ful.* This suffix means "full of." A reader can figure out that the meaning of *harmful* is "full of hurt or harm."

Synonyms, Antonyms, Homophones, Homographs, and Idioms

Synonyms and Antonyms

Synonyms are words that have similar or the same meaning. For example, *happy* and *glad* mean the same thing, so they are synonyms. A word may have many synonyms. Other synonyms for *happy* are *content* and *pleased*.

Antonyms are words that have opposite meanings. For example, *big* is an antonym for *small.* A word may have many antonyms. Other antonyms for *little* are *large* and *huge.*

Here are some common words with possible synonyms and antonyms:

Word	Synonym	Antonym
Fast	Quick	Slow
Loud	Noisy	Soft
Pretty	Beautiful	Ugly
Rich	Wealthy	Poor
Sick	Unwell	Healthy
Start	Begin	End
Tired	Sleepy	Energetic

Review Video: Synonyms and Antonyms
Visit mometrix.com/academy and enter code: 105612

Example

Determine if there is a synonym or an antonym for the word *silly* in the following sentence:

> Danny was so silly that his teacher had to keep reminding him to be serious and stop fooling around.

To figure out if there is a synonym for *silly*, the reader needs to look at the context of the sentence. A synonym means the same as another word. Danny's teacher reminds him to "stop fooling around." The sentence also says that Danny "was so silly." The term *fooling around* means almost the same as *silly*. The reader can tell this from the context clues because context clues are hints. An antonym means the opposite of another word. The teacher tells Danny "to be serious." The reader can figure out that *serious* means the opposite of *silly*. The reader can tell that *serious* is an antonym of *silly* because the context gives clues about the meaning of *serious* and *silly*.

Homographs and Homophones

There are several types of words that sound alike but that have different meanings. **Homographs** are words that are spelled the same way, but have different meanings and that aren't always pronounced the same way. **Homophones** are words that sound alike, but are spelled differently and have different meanings.

Because some words have many meanings, the reader has to decide which meaning of the word is being used. To figure out which meaning is being used, the reader needs to look for context clues to find hints about the meaning of the word. For example, the word *spot* is a homograph. It can mean "a place" or "a stain or blot." In the sentence "After my lunch, I saw a spot on my shirt," the word *spot* means "a stain or blot." Context clues help the reader figure this out. The hints include "lunch" and "on my shirt."

Homographs

Homographs	
Quarter	
It's a quarter past noon.	I put a quarter in the vending machine.
Bat	
I love to watch bats fly through the sky.	I had practice today, but I forgot my bat.
Left	
Look both right and left before you cross the road.	The plane left for New York at three o'clock.

Homophones

Homophones	
Bare	Bear
The trees already look bare.	These parks are full of bears.
Blue	Blew
My favorite color is blue.	My coffee was too hot, so I blew on it.
Be	Bee
Be careful in the parking lot!	Look at the bee on that flower!

Using Context to Determine the Meanings of Words

Readers of all levels will encounter words that they have either never seen or that they have seen before but still don't know what it means. The best way to define a word in **context** is to look for nearby words that can assist in learning the meaning of the word.

Context Clues

Context clues are hints about the meaning of a word. They are the words or phrases in the sentence or sentences before and after a new or unfamiliar word. Context clues give the reader an idea about what a word means. A context clue may also contain words that help define the new word or an example of what the new word means. sing context clues to figure out meaning can be helpful when learning a new set of vocabulary words or reading a difficult text. The dictionary definition of a word can always be looked up to double-check intended meaning.

Example

Read the following sentences and determine the meaning of the word *absorbed* based on context clues:

> Kamal was so *absorbed* by his video game that he didn't hear his grandmother calling him for dinner.

The dictionary definition of the word *absorbed* is "having one's attention fully engaged; greatly interested." In this sentence, the words "didn't hear" show that Kamal is not paying attention to anything other than what he's doing. The explanation that he's playing a video game tells us that he's most likely doing something he enjoys. The clues present in the sentence help the reader figure out that the word *absorbed* most likely means very interested. This word can also mean "liquid taken in or soaked up," but because Kamal is a person and not a liquid substance, the reader can determine that is not the correct meaning in this sentence.

Substitution to Find Meaning

One way to find out if you have figured out the correct meaning of a new word is to **substitute** the meaning for the word. Using the example for *absorbed*, if the reader substituted in "very interested," the sentence would read:

> Kamal was so "very interested" by his video game that he didn't hear his grandmother calling him for dinner.

This is a way for the reader to confirm that they have used the context clues in the sentence correctly.

Multiple-Meaning Words

A multiple-meaning word has different **definitions** in the dictionary. Many words have multiple meanings, so the reader has to pay attention to how a word is used in a sentence to figure out which meaning is intended. A multiple-meaning word is spelled the same, no matter how it is used. So, to find the meaning of a multiple-meaning word, the reader needs to look at the information presented in the rest of the sentence. For example, look at the word *leaves* in the following two sentences:

- Michelle *leaves* the building at 5 o'clock every day.
- The *leaves* fell off the oak tree in September.

In the first sentence, *leaves* means exits. In the second sentence, *leaves* refers to parts of a tree. By looking at the rest of each sentence, the reader can understand which definition of the multiple-meaning word the author is referring to.

Example

Figure out the meaning of the multi-meaning word *part* from the context of the following sentence:

> Anita wanted to have a *part* in figuring out when the school trip would take place.

Possible meanings of the word *part* include "piece," "quantity," and "role." The example sentence says that Anita wanted to have a *part* in figuring out when the school trip would take place." If the reader substitutes each meaning of the word *part* for the word itself, the reader can figure out that the correct meaning is "role." It is the only word that makes sense in this example sentence. Anita wanted to have a role in figuring out when the school trip would take place. "Role" is the correct meaning of *part* as used here.

Dictionary

A print or digital dictionary can be used to find out many things about a word. A dictionary will show the correct pronunciation of a word, provide its meaning, and identify what part of speech the word is. It will also tell how the word was derived—that is, what words it came from originally. A dictionary will have a **pronunciation guide** for each word that shows how to sound it out and where its syllables start and end. It will use symbols to indicate sounds, and will also use sample sounds (the "a" in "bad," for instance). A dictionary lists all of the meanings of a word and the parts of speech the word can be used as.

example \ ig-'zam-pəl\ noun
1. something that shows what a group of things is like
2. a model that should be either copied or avoided
3. a punishment meant to serve as a warning to others

EXAMPLE:

Julia used her dictionary to check the various meanings of the word *clear*. She found this entry:

clear (klîr) adjective
1. obvious.
2. easily seen through
3. free from flaw or blemish
4. free from guilt; untroubled
5. out of the way
6. to tidy *v*
7. to free *v*
8. to earn *v*

Identify which definition of *clear* is used in the following sentence:

Janet stood *clear* of the crowd pushing to get through the door.

The correct answer is meaning 5: "out of the way." If you substitute that definition for the word, the sentence makes sense. Meanings 1, 2, 3, and 4 do not fit with the context of the sentence. Meanings 6, 7, and 8 are verbs and "clear" as it is used in the sample is an adjective. When considering which meaning is being used, always check for context clues in the sentence or in the sentences before or after the sentence in which the word is used.

THESAURUS

A thesaurus is a reference book that gives **synonyms** of words. It is different from a dictionary because a thesaurus does not give definitions. A thesaurus can be helpful in finding the meaning of an unfamiliar word when reading. If the meaning of a synonym is known, then the meaning of the unfamiliar word will be known. Another time in which a thesaurus can be helpful is when writing. Using a thesaurus helps authors to vary their word choice.

GLOSSARY

A glossary is a **list of terms and their definitions** that can be found **at the back** of certain types of books, such as textbooks or reference books. A glossary does not have the definitions of all words, like a dictionary, but instead gives the definitions of the important terms within that particular book which are either uncommon or newly introduced. One may use a glossary when reading a book about economics or a chapter in a science textbook, for example, to define some of the technical terms within the text.

Author's Purpose

AUTHOR'S PURPOSE

An author may write a text for many different purposes. Four of the most common purposes are to inform, to persuade or influence, to express, or to entertain readers.

	Definition	Example
Informational Texts	Inform the reader on a topic that they previously knew nothing about, such as many non-fiction texts.	An informative paper on kangaroos would detail where kangaroos live, what they look like, what they eat, and other habits.
Persuasive Texts	Influence the reader to think a certain way about a topic, calling them to action or pointing them toward resources that would help them to learn more about the topic.	An author may try to persuade the reader that waterparks are the best place to go in the summer when it is hot outside. The author would present information about waterparks and explain *why* they are good places to visit.
Expressive Texts	Express the author or speaker's opinion or emotions about a topic. Lots of descriptive words are used to clearly show the reader how the author or speaker feels.	The author may think that a new playground in town is a good idea, and write an essay about why a playground would be great for the community.
Entertaining Texts	Entertain the reader, such as in most fictional texts.	Kate DiCamillo, the author of *Because of Winn Dixie*, entertains her readers with the story of a young girl named Opal and the stray dog who teaches Opal the meaning of friendship.

Authors usually write to entertain, to inform, or to persuade their readers. The organization structure or pattern they use is related to what the author's purpose is. It is important to choose the pattern that best presents the information, as not all patterns will work for every piece of writing.

EXAMPLE

Read the following sentence. State the author's point in writing the sentence, whether it is to inform, persuade, express an opinion, or entertain:

> The rollercoaster reached a peak and paused for a second, before gliding down the other side of the hill with a roar.

The purpose of the sentence is to entertain the reader. The author does not state his or her opinion on the topic, and the sentence doesn't inform the reader about an important topic. The sentence does not persuade the reader to accept a certain point of view, and is instead meant to entertain the reader by giving them the feeling they might get from riding an exciting roller coaster.

Notice that the text describes an event, rather than an issue or conflict. The event is part of a larger tale, where a series of events occur to form an entire story. The reader may notice that the author uses descriptive words to present the setting, such as gliding and roar. The reader can better picture a story when the setting is clearly presented.

Types of Texts

Fiction and Nonfiction

Nonfiction is anything that is based on factss, meaning that the content is true. Fiction is the opposite, so any story that is made up, even if it seems real, is actually fiction. **Fiction** does not have to include imaginary ideas like dragons and aliens, but can include realistic stories.

Examples of Fiction and Nonfiction

Fiction	Nonfiction
A book about kids who go to a school for magic.	A book describing how magic has been seen throughout history.
A cartoon depicting a caterpillar eating various foods.	An article describing the eating habits of caterpillars.
A story about a made up man going to the moon.	A story about a real person who went to the moon.

Main Idea and Supporting Details

Controlling Idea

The **controlling idea**, also called the **main idea** or thesis, of a passage is usually located in the first paragraph or two of text. Having the controlling idea near the beginning of the passage allows the author to grab the reader's attention and let them know what the rest of the passage will discuss.

To find the controlling idea in a passage, there are questions the reader can ask while reading: What is this passage about? What does the author want the reader to know about the topic? The supporting details will provide evidence that the controlling idea is correct and are found in the body of a passage. The supporting details often provide examples of the controlling idea.

Supporting Details

Supporting details provide evidence and backing for the controlling idea. All texts contain details, but they are only classified as supporting details when they serve to reinforce some larger point. Supporting details are most commonly found in informative and persuasive texts. In some cases, they will be clearly indicated with words like for example or for instance, or they will be enumerated with words like first, second, and last. However, these special words are not a requirement. As a reader, it is important to consider whether the author's supporting details really back up his or her main point. Supporting details can be factual and correct but still not relevant to the author's point. Sometimes, supporting details can seem important but they might not support the main idea in the story well because they are based on opinion that cannot be proven.

Example

Read the following two sentences. State which sentence is a main idea and which sentence is a supporting detail. Explain the difference between the two sentences:

> She went fishing with her cousin Vinny.
>
> Jayden visited her relatives in Louisiana over the summer.

The first sentence is a supporting detail, and the second sentence is the main idea. A main idea gives the overall concept, or point, of the story. A supporting detail adds more information to the point of the story. The reader already knows that the name of the character needs to be introduced before using the pronoun she. Therefore, it makes sense that Jayden visiting her relatives in Louisiana over the summer must come before the supporting detail about her going fishing with her cousin Vinny. Once the reader knows the overall point of the text, supporting details help to explain what else happens in the story. The reader knows from the main point that the character Jayden is visiting her relatives in Louisiana, which is where she went fishing.

EXAMPLE

Read the following main idea of a story and write a supporting detail for it:

> Madison's favorite thing to talk about was strawberries.

A good supporting detail would need to include information that supports or explains more about the main idea. A supporting detail might read: "She also loved to eat them," or "She also grew strawberries in her backyard." Supporting details provide additional information about the main idea that has not already been presented to the reader. A supporting detail further develops the topic of the story and provides an explanation of a part of the main idea.

In the example supporting details above, note that the topic is still focused on the subject of strawberries and action that the character takes in relation to that particular subject. A main idea will often appear in the first one to two paragraphs of a story. Supporting details appear later in a paragraph or in other paragraphs within the story.

KEY IDEAS AND SUPPORTING DETAILS

Identifying **key ideas** helps the reader see what a text or story is mostly about. They are the **most important ideas** in a text, and everything else in the text builds around and supports them. Every piece of writing has key ideas. The **supporting details** in a story, such as the characters, events, and settings, will work together to reveal the key ideas. The details are not key ideas, themselves. They make the key ideas clear and show the reader the author's purpose for writing the text.

THEME

The **theme** of a story, essay, or poem is the lesson that it teaches, or the message the author wants to get across. The theme is linked to the characters, the setting, and the events in a story. Some themes are fairly common. These themes are called **universal themes** and they suggest things about life, society, and human nature.

The theme of a story is not the same as the topic of a story. The topic is what the story is about, but the theme is what a reader is meant to learn. Themes are very rarely stated in the text. Instead, the reader has to **infer** the theme by reading closely and thinking carefully about what the author is saying.

Themes are an important part of literature because they serve the purpose of teaching the reader or listener a truth about life. The theme is developed by how a character or characters respond to their situations and challenges.

EXAMPLE

Read the following and consider the theme of the excerpt.

> Jeanie arrived at the bake sale early. She bought the biggest cake at the sale. Sally had to work late. When she finally got to the sale, no cakes were left. She got only two cookies. She was lucky to get anything.

The saying "the early bird gets the worm" is one way to explain the theme of the story. In the story we read that Jeanie arrived early at the bake sale and got the biggest cake. But when Sally arrived, all that was left were two cookies. The point of the story is that the early bird gets the worm—the worm in this case is a large cake. In this story, the topic is a bake sale, but the theme is not "bake sale" because the words "bake sale" do not teach the reader anything.

Making Inferences

MAKING INFERENCES

In a fictional work of literature, there are things that the author does not actually say, but hints at; the reader needs to connect the dots of these clues to draw a conclusion. This is called making an **inference**. An inference is a conclusion that the reader makes using clues in the text. An inference is different from making a guess, because inferences are based on evidence and guesses are random. When asked to infer something, the reader needs to use specific details from the text to show that their answer is supported.

For example, an author might mention that a character has a messy room and papers falling out of his binder. The reader can infer that the character is sloppy and disorganized even though the author does not **explicitly** state this fact.

Personal experience also helps a reader draw a conclusion. For example, suppose there is a story about two girls going to a movie. In the story, the girls are laughing at the end of the movie. This information helps a reader draw a conclusion, because they have likely laughed at a movie before. The conclusion is that the movie is funny. This may not be the reason the girls are laughing, but it seems likely. If the story said the girls had tears in their eyes at the end of the movie, a reader might conclude that the movie is sad.

EXAMPLE

Describe what conclusion can be drawn based on the following sentences:

> Mr. Ted E. Bear was a hungry dog. He loved to eat his breakfast and his dinner. He would lap up his food in just minutes. One day his master forgot to feed him dinner because he had to meet someone. As the dog's master left, he noticed a sandwich on the table. When he got back, the sandwich was gone.

Conclusions are made based on the information in a story. A reader needs to find clues to form a conclusion about a story. This is a story about a hungry dog. The dog loves to eat. He is fed in the morning and the evening. His master forgets to feed him. His master goes out and leaves a sandwich on a table. When he comes back, the sandwich is gone. The conclusion a reader will draw is that the dog ate the sandwich. That is the most likely thing that happened to it. It may not be correct, but based on the information, it is the best conclusion.

EXAMPLE

Describe what can be inferred from the following sentences:

> Sometimes after a big storm, the beaches are covered with dead fish, seaweed, broken shells, and pieces of wood. Most seaweed is brown or gold, but there are often pieces of white seaweed. If people visit the beaches, the white seaweed disappears very quickly. It makes a delicious pudding.

To make an inference a reader needs to look for clues in a text. The author does not tell an inference directly; the author hints at one. Here the text says that fish, seaweed, and shells are on the beach after a storm. It also says that some of the seaweed is white and adds that the white seaweed is used for pudding. Another clue is that the white seaweed disappears quickly if people visit the beaches. The inference that a reader can figure out is that the people take the seaweed. It disappears quickly because it can be used to make a delicious pudding.

EXAMPLE

Read the following sentences and decide what evidence supports the conclusion that Tommy wasn't getting enough sleep:

> Tommy liked to sleep in his own bed. He had a hard time falling asleep in any other bed. Last week he visited his cousin. He stayed over for the weekend. At first, they had fun, but by the end of the weekend, Tommy was tired and grouchy. He wanted to go home.

The conclusion is that Tommy wasn't getting enough sleep. A reader needs to look for the evidence that the conclusion is true. A reader needs to find clues that support the conclusion. The story says that Tommy liked to sleep in his own bed and that he had trouble falling asleep in other beds. He visited his cousin for the weekend and ended up tired and grouchy. There are details in the story that support the conclusion that Tommy wasn't getting enough sleep. The detail that Tommy had a hard time falling asleep in another bed is one. The detail that Tommy was tired and grouchy at the end of the weekend is another.

GENERATING QUESTIONS ABOUT TEXTS BEFORE, DURING, AND AFTER READING

Asking questions during the process of reading is one way for you to become a more **active reader**. Active readers do not just sit back and have the content handed to them. Instead, they get involved with the text and are part of the process of learning. Asking questions before you read, pausing to ask questions while you're reading, and asking questions after you read are all good ways to help you become a more active reader. There are three types of questioning that can use as you try to think of questions.

QUESTIONING YOURSELF

These are questions you ask yourself to see how well you're paying attention, and how involved you are in the story. Some example questions are

- Which character is my favorite so far?
- What do I think is going to happen next?
- Is there a character I am similar to in this story? Do I like those similarities?
- What would I do if I was in this situation?

QUESTIONING THE AUTHOR

Although the chances are slim that you will ever get the chance to meet most of the authors of the texts you read, another way to get involved in the text is to imagine that you are asking questions of the author him or herself. Some example questions are

- What did the author want me to see here?
- Why did he write about this subject?
- Why did the author use this phrase?
- What did she want the character to learn from this?

Questioning the Text

The last type of question you can ask to improve your reading is called questioning the text. To ask these questions, imagine that you are asking the text itself questions about how it works and what it means. Some examples are:

- What does this word mean?
- What is this paragraph describing?
- Why is this term used here?
- How does this sentence connect to the other sentences in this paragraph?

Summarizing Information

Paraphrasing and Summarizing

Paraphrasing and summarizing are two ways readers can work to understand what they read. Both involve reading a text and recalling the main points in an accurate way, but they differ in several ways.

How to Paraphrase	How to Summarize
State the message in the text in the reader's own words, while keeping the original meaning of the text Take all of the original ideas and word them in a way that the reader can better understand Put what the reader has read into their own words, rephrasing what the author has written	State main points of the text clearly and to-the-point. Take information and state it simply, in a much shorter form. Put information in a short form that keeps the main points of the whole text. Do not include many details, just the main idea of the text

Paraphrasing is often done for individual ideas, while summarizing is done for an entire block of text or ideas. Often times, a summary can be done in just one sentence, boiling down the author's words into just main idea.

Paraphrasing the Main Point of a Sentence

Paraphrase the main point of the following two sentences:

> Emmanuel went swimming in the lake by his house, where the water reached a depth of twenty feet in the middle. He did not venture out more than six feet into the water, however.

When paraphrasing a couple sentences or an entire paragraph, always include the main point of the text being reviewed, this is what the reader needs to know about the text. In the example, the reader needs to know that Emmanuel went swimming in the lake, but not more than six feet out. A paraphrase of the text may include: Emmanuel went swimming six feet out in the lake by his house. That is the main point that the audience needs to know.

Recall that a paraphrase is stating the author's ideas in the reader's own words. A summary typically involves including the main points of a longer text, such as a novel or full story.

Example

Read the following paragraph and then give a one sentence summary statement:

> When choosing a pet, people need to think about what type of home they can offer the animal. For example, a small apartment might not be a good fit for a large dog, but could be a comfortable home for a kitten. A house that has a big yard would be great for a puppy, but a rabbit does not need a large yard.

In order to summarize, one has to identify the main idea and any supporting ideas in the author's work. The summary is an overview of the author's paragraph and will tell what it is about without getting into any of the details. The summary needs to be broad enough to cover all of the information in the author's paragraph. Here is a possible summary statement for the above paragraph:

> People need to consider a number of factors when choosing a pet.

Elements of Story

Setting

The setting is where a story **takes place**. The setting of a story may stay the same for the entire story, or change as events in the story unfold. For example, an entire story may take place in one room, or on the other end, a story could cross continents as the reader follows the characters along on a trail of events. Every story has to take place somewhere. The setting of story is described by the author in terms of what it looks like, how the character feels, and anything that is happening at that location at the time. For example, a character may be caught on a doorstep on a cold, rainy day. The character may feel frustrated as he shivers in the doorway, waiting for the heavy rain to let up a bit.

Example

When listing ways that a story set in the city has a different backdrop from a story set in the countryside, answers will vary based on current knowledge of common characteristics for each setting. A story set in a city may be different from a story set in the countryside based on the following factors:

- Number of passersby: many people on a sidewalk vs. no other people around
- Background noise: car horns vs. bird calls
- Types of surroundings: tall buildings vs. fields of corn
- Types of transportation: subways and taxis vs. horses and farm trucks
- Daily activities being carried out: sitting at a desk in a skyscraper vs. plowing fields for planting
- Type of attire: a business suit vs. dirty jeans and boots

Shaping a Character with Setting or Plot

The setting of a story shapes character because it helps to define the situation that a character finds herself in. A character is limited to the setting of a story. For example, if a story takes place in a cold environment filled with snow and ice, this is certain to impact what actions a character can and will take. Frequently, the setting changes the way characters behave based on time. For example, the character of a woman who is a single mother in 1920 would be seen and behave very differently than a single mother in 2020.

Example

Read the excerpt and determine how the setting influences the character in this excerpt.

> She had swum too far out. The waves were higher than she thought. She was struggling hard to get to shore. She wondered if she would make it. She thought of her childhood. Had she been right to run away from home, she wondered? Just then, a lifeguard grabbed her and helped her to shore.

The setting of the ocean and the high waves creates a conflict in the character. She is worried. She thinks about her childhood and her parents. She doesn't know if she will make it to shore. This is how the setting affects the character in this excerpt. Without the high waves and the struggle, she would not become so worried and start to think about her past. She probably would not have questioned herself. This is an example of how a setting influences a character. If the waves had not been high, there probably would not have been a struggle or any self-searching of the swimmer's past.

Style and Voice

Style and voice play an important role in the development of a story. The reader's impression of a story can vary based on the style and voice used by the author. **Style** refers to the way an author uses words, phrases, and sentence structure. The style of the text can change depending on whether the author uses short, choppy sentences, long, elaborate sentences, formal language, or informal language. **Voice** refers to the characteristics of a text that show the author's personality and distinguish the author from other writers. An author's voice may be recognized through the way they use words or the way they organize and present their thoughts. Voice is specific to each writer, and it can be as specific and unique as personality.

Point of View

Authors choose which character tells the story they are writing. This is called **point of view**. The point of view affects the story in many ways. There are three general types of point of view:

First Person

- Tells a story through the eyes of one character.
- Uses the pronouns 'I,' 'me,' 'we,' and 'my.'
- The reader gets only one side of the story, without any other angles on what may have happened in the text

Second Person

- Tells a story using the pronoun 'you.'
- The least common point of view.

Third Person

- Tells a story about a character or group of characters from an outside viewpoint.
- Uses the words 'her', 'his,' 'they,' or a name to talk about a character or characters.
- A common way to show action in a story which allows the author to easily and realistically tell a story from more than one person's viewpoint.
- Gives readers a more complete view of a story as it is told from many different perspectives.

Plot

The term **plot** refers to the series of events that take place in a story. The events in a story may take place in one location or many, in a short amount of time or over many years. A story always has to start somewhere, and the first event in a story signals the beginning of the plot. Stories may vary in length from half a page to novel-length, but they all follow a progression of events that the author winds together to form the plot. The characters and events in the story determine what the plot will be. Readers may find a **plot line** useful as they try to put the events in the text in order and determine the relationships between events.

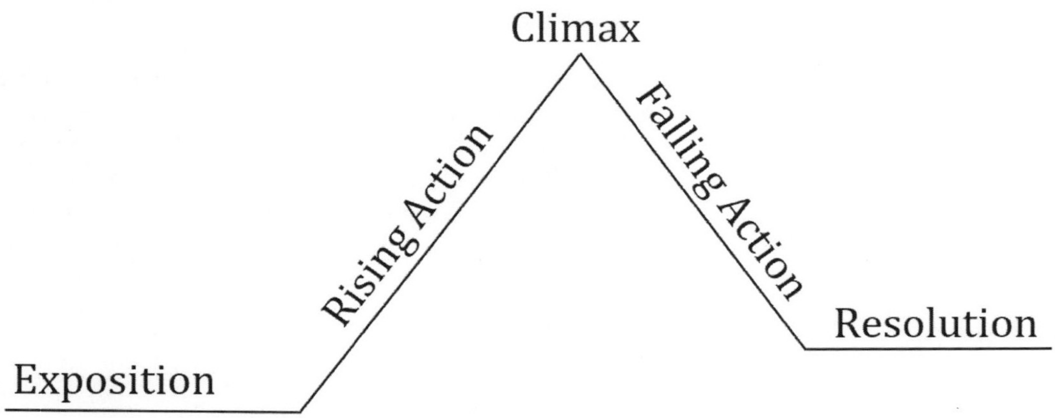

Review Video: Plot Line
Visit mometrix.com/academy and enter code: 944011

Every plot will begin with **exposition**, which introduces the characters and the setting of the story. The plot will continue to develop as new ideas and events centered on the main conflict in the story are revealed, which is called the **rising action**. The action in the story will rise until a **climax** is reached within the conflict. The climax can also be referred to as the turning point in the story, since the climax is where each character makes an important decision. After the climax, the action starts to wind down during the **falling action**. At this point, the characters begin to follow the paths they chose in during climax. The events of the story reach **resolution** in some way by the end of the story. Some conflicts are left open-ended, so that the reader is left to decide what really happened at the end of the story. Keep in mind that not all resolutions are happy or peaceful.

EXAMPLE

Read the following plot and determine what the missing event is in the plot sequence:

> Sarita went to the store to buy eggs for her mother. She bought the eggs and got back on her bicycle to bring the eggs home. Her mother was angry that the eggs were all broken.

The reader has to guess based on the plot sequence what happened between events. The reader knows that Sarita got on her bicycle to go home. The reader also knows that the eggs were broken when she arrived at the house. Based on the context, the reader can assume that Sarita fell off her bicycle or dropped the eggs on the way home, causing them to all be broken when she arrived. The reader can assume that Sarita would have noticed if the eggs were already broken in the store. Plot often follows a logical sequence of events, but sometimes it is difficult to decide what actually happened between two events. In the example, the reader can logically assume that the eggs were broken on the way home.

Conflict

Conflict creates the basis for the plot of a story. A conflict may be between characters, a character and their own mind, or an outside influence. The main point of a conflict is that there is a problem that needs to be resolved. The problem may be a disagreement or an obstacle that has arisen and needs to be overcome.

An important part of analyzing the plot of a passage is identifying the **main conflict**. There will likely be many smaller conflicts in the story, but there will be one main problem that influences the characters and events. To identify the main conflict, first look at who the main character is. Now ask yourself what they want. They may want to something to happen or not happen, another character to do or not do something, or to confront or avoid a problem, among other things. Once you know what they want, now ask yourself what is standing in the character's way. It may be a person, an event, or something less tangible like the passing of time. Combining what the main character wants and why they do not currently have leaves the reader with a summary of the main conflict.

Example

Read the following sentence and explain the main conflict between the two characters:

> Joe stared angrily at Jamie's retreating back as Jamie raced away down the field with Joe's soccer ball.

The main conflict in the sentence is that Jamie has Joe's soccer ball. There may be additional conflicts between the two characters, but none are evident from the evidence shown in the sentence. In any story, a conflict may be minor and only affect part of the story, or be the main focus, taking an entire story to solve a conflict between characters. In the context of the sentence, it is not clear whether or not the entire story will revolve around Jamie taking Joe's soccer ball.

Resolution

The term **resolution** usually indicates the result of a conflict in a story. Conflict between characters, within a character, or against an external element is necessary in order to have a plot for a story. Without conflict, no events would occur to form the story. A conflict will come to a climax, and then conclude in some way. The resolution of a problem may be open-ended, end tragically, or end in a way that is good for everyone involved. The problem resolution typically occurs near the end of a story, after the climax has happened. A problem may be resolved by the characters involved within the conflict or by an external event; an upcoming resolution may be foreshadowed in the text, or may be completely unexpected by the reader. If the resolution is completely unexpected, it is considered to be a **twist** in the story.

Characters

Character Relationships

A relationship is the way one character acts with another character in a story. The characters are often called **major characters** if they have a main part in the story and **minor characters** if they have a smaller part. There are many different kinds of relationships. For example, two children in a story may be friends, but they could be angry with each other, competing with each other, or helping each other. An author may tell the reader what kind of relationship the characters have. An author might give hints about a relationship. For example, the author may show one child making fun of the other child, which would suggest that the two children do not have a friendly relationship. The author might show one child teaching the other child how to read, which would suggest that the two children have a friendly relationship.

EXAMPLE

Read the following sentences and describe the relationship Jill and Anna have:

> Jill came over to Anna and asked if she wanted an apple. "Sure, I'd love one. Thanks," Anna answered. Anna took a bite of the apple and started to chew it. Her chewing was so loud that they both started to laugh.

The author does not tell what the relationship between Jill and Anna is. The reader must figure it out from their actions. These actions are the clues the author gives. Jill asks Anna if she wants an apple. Anna says yes and starts to eat it. Her chewing is very loud. Both Jill and Anna start to laugh. They seem to like each other. Jill seems generous to Anna because she gives Anna an apple. They laugh together, and friends often laugh together. The reader can use personal experience to decide that it seems as though Jill and Anna are friends.

CHARACTERS' FEELINGS

An author can show how a character feels in many ways. For example, the character may laugh a lot, which shows that the character is happy. The character could cry, which shows that the character is sad. There are other ways an author shows a character's feelings. A character may say something that shows he or she is sad. For example, a character may say that she misses her old school. This statement would show that the character is sad. A character may say something about enjoying her new school. This statement would show that the character is happy. An author knows that a character's feelings are important in a story. Sometimes the author says how a character is feeling; other times the author gives hints or clues about what a character feels.

EXAMPLE

Read the following sentences and describe how Lorna feels:

> Lorna walked forward very slowly. The strange scratching noise was growing louder. She thought about calling out for help, but she knew no one would hear her. She decided to keep going anyway.

The author does not tell the reader directly how Lorna feels, but there are many clues about how Lorna feels from her actions. The sentences say that Lorna walks forward slowly and that there is a strange scratching noise. The sentence also says that she thinks about calling for help. These clues all suggest that Lorna is frightened. She doesn't know what is making the scratching noise. She wants to call for help, but she cannot. She is scared. The sentences also suggest another feeling. Lorna doesn't run away. She decides to keep going. This is another clue. It shows that Lorna is also feeling brave.

EFFECT OF PLOT ON A STORY'S CHARACTERS

The plot of a story unfolds as each event follows another, shaping the characters as they react to the various events that occur. Some characters are able to resolve their problems by the end of the story, while some characters fail to overcome their predicaments. As characters respond to the events around them, they reveal more and more about their personalities. Some grow and some do not. The reader can use the events of the plot to interpret the meaning of the story and understand its characters.

Example

Read the excerpt and explain how finding the chest affects Marta.

> The map said this was the spot. Marta held her breath. Her fists were clenched into two tight balls. She lifted the shovel and scooped more sand out of the hole. There it was; she had found the chest with the diamonds. She opened the top. She would never need to work again. She smiled. It was really happening.

The event affects Marta by making her happy. The reader gets several clues that she is anxiously waiting ("Marta held her breath" and "her fists were clenched"), and that she is happy with what she found ("She smiled"). Events can cause characters to have all kinds of feelings. Here, something wonderful happened. However, events in stories are not always quite so happy. For instance, if a robber had suddenly seen Marta and the chest, he might have stolen the chest. That event would have had a very different effect on her. Readers need to pay attention to how characters are reacting to events, whether they are simply hinted at or stated in the story. In this way a reader will learn what characters are like.

Text Features

Print and Graphic Features

An author may show information in a chart, a graph, in paragraph format, or as a list. Information may also be shown in a picture or a diagram. The way an author chooses to show information is often based on the purpose of the text and the audience that the text is meant to reach.

A reader may be asked to answer questions based on the graphic by itself, how the graphic relates to the text, or how the text would best be shown in a graphic form. Some common examples of graphics are cause and effect organizers, circle graphs, bar graphs, illustrations, and diagrams.

Cause and Effect Graphic Organizers

Cause-and-effect graphic organizers are often used to map the **elements of a story**. A reader might read a story about a string of events and then be asked to correctly fill in either the **cause** or **effect** of an event in the story.

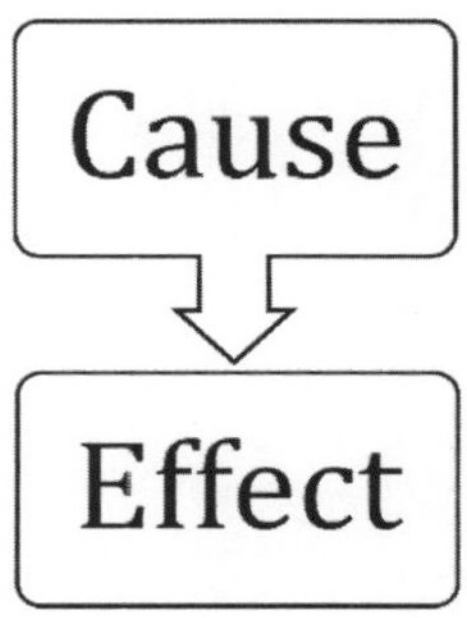

EXAMPLE

Read the following excerpt from *Ramona Quimby, Age 8* by Beverly Cleary and decide what the cause of the hectic morning at the Quimby house is.

> With all four members of the family leaving at different times in different directions, mornings were flurried in the Quimby household.

A **cause and effect** graphic organizer for this excerpt might look something like this:

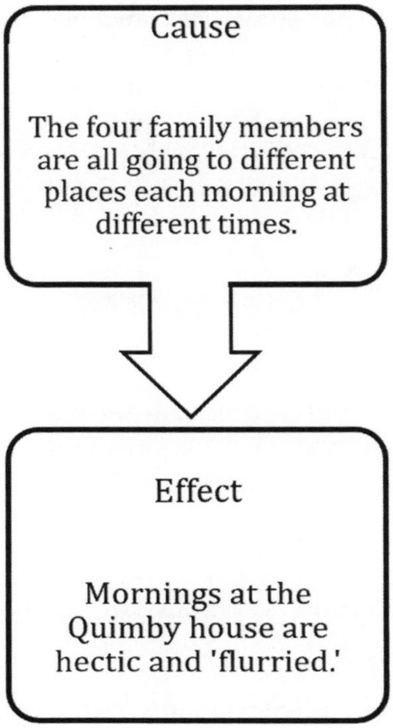

Circle Graphs

Circle graphs, also called pie charts, are often used to represent information that can be shown as **parts of a whole**. For example, this graph shows the results of people being asked about their favorite color:

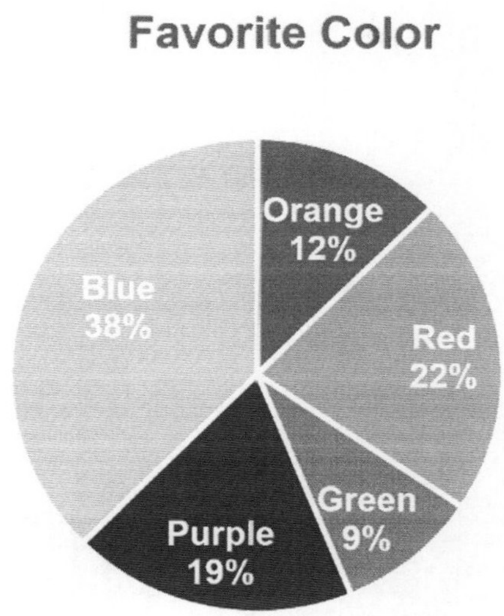

Bar Graphs

Bar graphs are used to show information about **numbers**. For example, this graph is a different way of representing the same results as those in the circle graph.

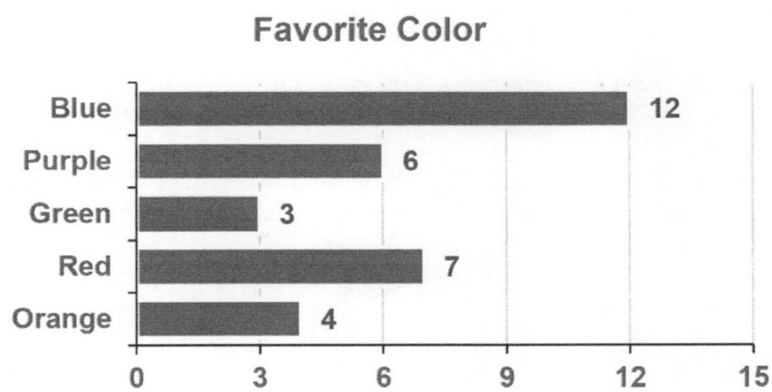

Illustrations and Photographs

Authors may choose to include **illustrations** or **photographs** (or both) with their texts. These two image types both show something from the text or give more information about the text.

Illustrations are drawings of an object. They may be based on reality, or they may represent an artist's abstract idea. For example, this is an illustration of a 1903 automobile:

Photographs are pictures of objects. They are generally extremely realistic, and most often show an object as it actually existed at that moment in time. For example, this is a photograph of a 1917 automobile:

Both illustrations and photographs give the reader another way to relate to and understand the text. The reader may be asked how the image relates to the text, what type of caption the image should be given, or why the author chose to include the image with the text.

DIAGRAMS

Diagrams are used to show information in a visual way. There are many different types of diagrams, including:

Diagrams that show the parts of an object, how they work together, or how they should be put together. This is an example of a diagram which shows how gears turn together

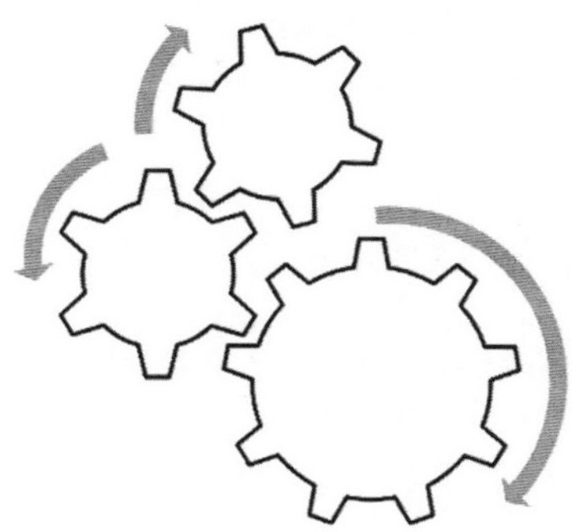

Diagrams that show how information is related are called **Venn Diagrams**. These are ways to visually see the way in which two different ideas overlap. This is an example of a Venn Diagram comparing cats and dogs:

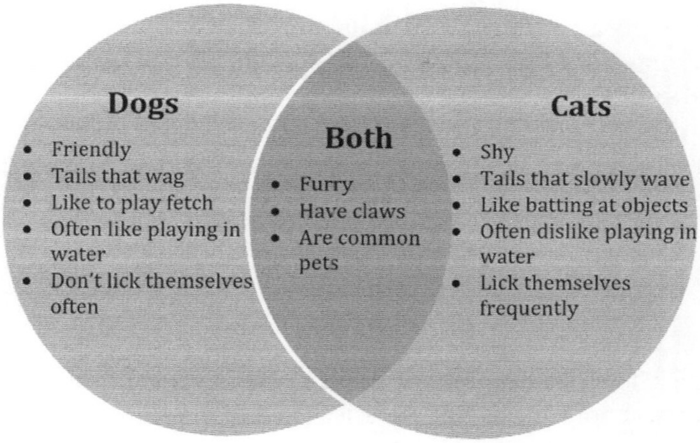

Making Predictions

Predicting What Will Happen in a Story

When you read a story, you should look for clues to make a prediction about what will happen. At the end of the story, you may even think about what will happen next to the main character, and use the clues in the story to make a prediction. You can also use personal experience to help make a prediction.

Suppose there is a story about a boy going swimming, and he swims too far out. Suppose the story says the boy can't get back to shore and starts to yell. Suppose the lifeguard comes and helps him. Suppose the story stops after the boy goes back in the water again. The reader might make the prediction that the boy won't swim as far out this time. This may not be true, but it is the most likely thing to happen.

Example

Describe what prediction can be made based on the following sentences:

> When Glen is sick, his mother keeps him home from school. He stays in bed all day and takes medicine. Glen woke up this morning with a sore throat. His head was hot, and he felt achy.

The story says that Glen's mother keeps him home when he is sick and that Glen spends the day in bed when he is sick. The story says that Glen woke up this morning with a sore throat. His head was hot, and he felt achy. The reader can figure out that Glen was sick. Because Glen's mother always keeps him home when he is sick, the reader can predict that Glen will be staying home from school and spending the day in bed.

You can also use text features find information to make predictions and verify conclusions determined about different texts. Using key words as clues, looking for bold print words, looking for sentences that include captions, and words that are written in italics are a few features that can be used to help understand and make predictions about a text.

USING STRUCTURE AND GENRE TO MAKE PREDICTIONS

The structure and genre of a story can also help readers make predictions. Most stories follow the same structure. They have an exposition, rising action, a climax, falling action, and a resolution. Because most stories follow this structure, readers can predict that each of these parts will occur in the story. For example, rising action usually begins after the conflict of the story is introduced. This means that if characters have not faced any conflict, the reader can predict that something will go wrong for the characters. Likewise, stories in the same genre may contain similar events. For example, in a mystery, the characters work to solve a crime or explain a strange event. So, when reading a mystery, the reader can predict that the conflict will be a crime or event that the characters must learn more about.

Text Evidence and Drawing Conclusions

TEXT EVIDENCE

The term **text evidence** refers to information found in a text that supports a reader's claim about the text. A reader can draw conclusions or inferences based upon information found in a text. Often, the author will deliberately include information that supports the main point of the text to help the reader make conclusions and inferences that align with the author's purpose for writing the text.

DRAWING CONCLUSIONS BASED ON TEXT EVIDENCE

Readers often need to use prior experience and background information to draw an accurate conclusion about the passage they are reading. Sometimes interpreting the information in a sentence can be difficult, especially if the reader is unfamiliar with some of the words used in a sentence. Looking at the words that the reader does understand in the sentence can help. By taking a pen or pencil and underlining important information in a sentence, the reader can better understand what the author is trying to say and draw a clearer conclusion from that.

EXAMPLE

Draw a conclusion based on the following quote from *Flora & Ulysses: The Illuminated Adventures* by Kate DiCamillo

> Take this squirrel, for instance. Ulysses. Do I believe he can type poetry? Sure, I do believe it. There is much more beauty in the world if I believe such a thing is possible.

This quote is from the character Dr. Meescham, who is speaking to Flora about her squirrel, Ulysses. Saying a squirrel can type seems silly, but the doctor says he does believe it's true. The phrase "there is much more beauty... if I believe" helps the reader draw the conclusion that Dr. Meescham encourages imagination, and that seeing the world as beautiful is important. The things characters say often show something important about them. Be sure to read dialogue carefully to see what conclusions the author might be wanting you to make.

EXAMPLE

Read the following quote from *Shiloh* by Phyliss Reynolds Naylor and draw a conclusion based upon the information presented.

> Last of all, I take the lard bread from my pocket and feed it to Shiloh in little pieces, letting him lick my fingers after every bite. I wrap my arms around him, pat him, run my hands over his ears, even kiss his nose. I tell him about a million times I love him as much as I love my ma.

The reader can conclude that the narrator adores his dog Shiloh. The words "wrap my arms around him," "kiss his nose," and "tell him about a million times I love him" lead the reader to this conclusion. The reader can also assume that Shiloh loves the narrator as well because he allows all of the touches that he is receiving. Readers know from experience that animals do not often allow touch from people they do not have affection for.

When interpreting a sentence, always look for key phrases that can be used to draw conclusions about characters and their relationships. Authors carefully craft descriptions of each character to form a picture in the reader's mind about what the character is like.

Connecting with Texts

MAKING CONNECTIONS TO ENHANCE COMPREHENSION

Reading involves thinking. For good comprehension, readers make text-to-self, text-to-text, and text-to-world connections. Making connections helps readers understand text better and predict what might occur next based on what they already know, such as how characters in the story feel or what happened in another text. Readers can make connections before, during, and after reading. Venn diagrams and other graphic organizers can help readers visualize connections.

TEXT-TO-SELF

Reading while looking for connections with the reader's life and experiences makes literature more personally relevant and meaningful to readers. Sentences showing text-to-self connections may begin with these examples

- This reminds me of a time when...
- I understand how the character feels because...
- The setting makes me think of...
- I experienced this same thing when...

TEXT-TO-TEXT

Reading while looking for connections to other texts helps the reader learn to identify the way authors use genre, setting, characters, plot elements, literary structure and devices, and themes to create meaning. Sentences showing text-to-text connections may begin with these examples

- The character in this story reminds me of the character in...
- These two stories are alike because...
- The conflict in this story is similar to the conflict in...
- The relationship between the friends in this story is different than the relationship in...

TEXT-TO-WORLD

Reading while looking for connections to the world helps the reader begin to see literature as a reflection of real life and notice patterns in history and current events. Sentences showing text-to-world connections may begin with these examples

- The event in this story sounds like the event in history when...
- The actions of this character sound like...
- This is like what happened in real life when...
- I heard about this on the news when...

Math Practice Test #1

1. Arlan compares his annual electricity expenses over a five-year time span. His annual expenses are shown in the table below.

Year	Expense
2007	$1,224
2008	$1,319
2009	$1,046
2010	$1,529
2011	$1,342

Which of the following shows the years listed, in order, from lowest electricity expense to highest electricity expense?

a. 2009, 2008, 2007, 2010, 2011
b. 2007, 2009, 2011, 2010, 2008
c. 2009, 2007, 2011, 2008, 2010
d. 2009, 2007, 2008, 2011, 2010

2. Steve had to pay a library fee. The amount he paid is shown below.

How much did he pay?

a. $2.84
b. $2.59
c. $2.74
d. $2.69

3. Wyatt's coach passed out balls to the entire team. One-third of the balls Wyatt received were basketballs. Which of the following could represent the balls he received?

a. 

b. 

c. 

d. 

4. An author had a book published last year. The number of books sold each month, for the first six months are: 321, 452, 608, 381, 294, and 458.

Which of the following lists the number of books sold each month, in order from greatest to least?

a. 608, 452, 458, 321, 384, 294
b. 452, 458, 608, 381, 321, 294
c. 458, 608, 452, 381, 321, 294
d. 608, 458, 452, 381, 321, 294

5. Students were given triangles and hexagons to be used during a class activity. One-third of the shapes each student received were triangles. Which of the following could represent the number of triangles and number of hexagons each student received?

a. 

b. 

c. 

d. 

6. What number sentence is illustrated by the diagram below?

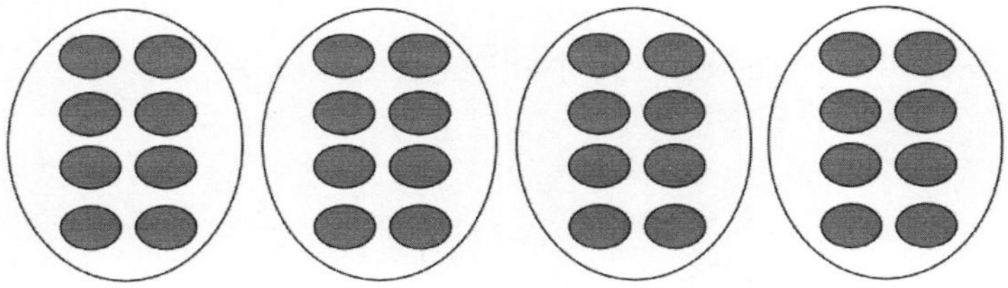

a. $32 \times 4 = 128$
b. $32 - 4 = 28$
c. $32 \div 4 = 8$
d. $32 + 4 = 36$

7. Solve and place answer on the provided griddable sheet.

$$\begin{array}{r} 96 \\ \times\ 5 \\ \hline \end{array}$$

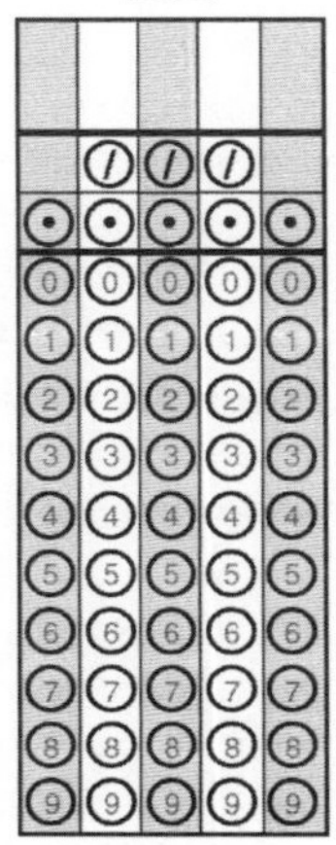

8. Edward ascends to the top of a mountain over the course of two days. On Friday, he ascends 482 feet. He ascends another 362 feet on Saturday. How many feet did he ascend in all?

a. 848 feet
b. 836 feet
c. 840 feet
d. 844 feet

9. Kristen must buy two items that are priced at \$62, and \$89. What is the best estimate for the total cost of both items?

a. \$120
b. \$150
c. \$200
d. \$180

10. Which of the following represents $\frac{2}{3}$?

a. 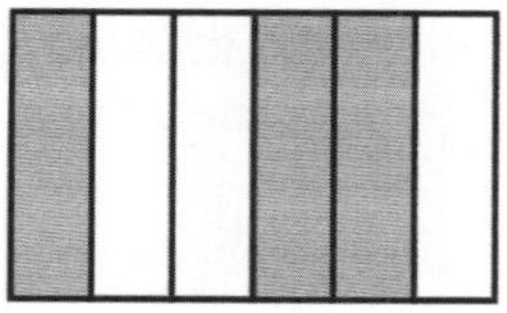

b. 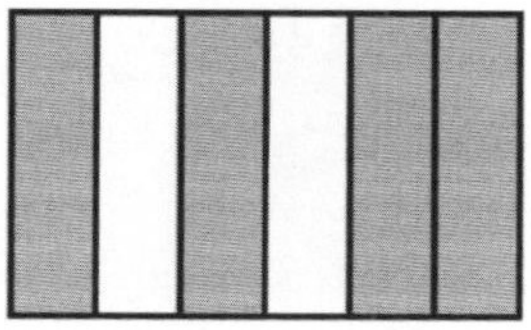

c. 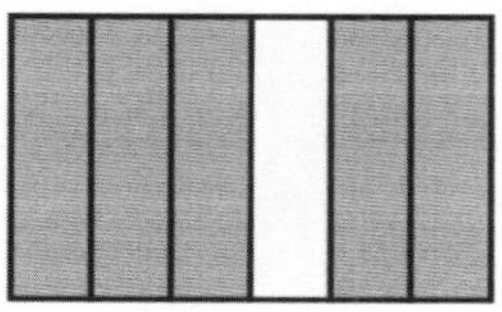

d. 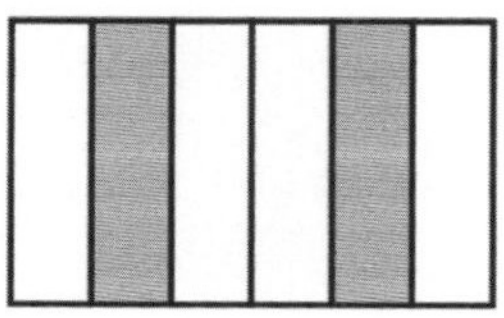

11. On Monday, David finished gluing 96 tiles in 8 hours. On Tuesday, he finished gluing 72 tiles in 8 hours. Which of the following is a possible first step in determining how many more tiles he glued per hour on Monday?

a. Add the number of tiles glued each day
b. Subtract the number of hours it took to glue the tiles from the number of tiles glued
c. Multiply the number of hours spent gluing tiles on Monday by the number of hours spent gluing tiles on Tuesday
d. Divide the number of tiles glued each day by the number of hours it took to glue them

12. Solve and place answer on the provided griddable sheet.

At the birthday party, each guest received 12 game tokens and each game takes 2 tokens. If there were 9 guests at the party, estimate how many games were played (to the nearest tens)?

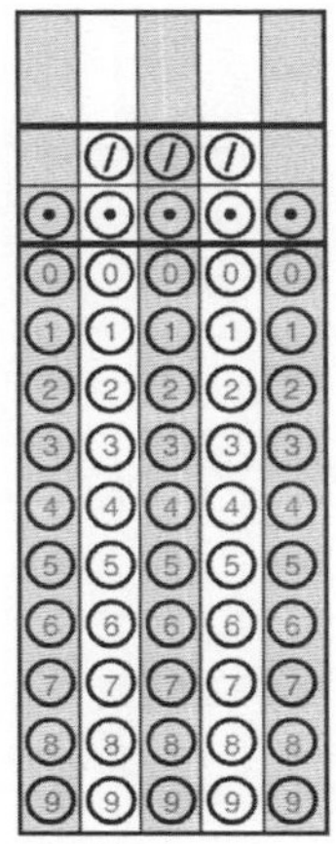

13. What is the eighth number in the pattern: 321, 329, 337, 345, ___, ___, ___, ___?

a. 369
b. 385
c. 377
d. 353

14. A little boy has three nickels, four dimes, two pennies, and two quarters. How much money does he have?

a. $1.00
b. $0.90
c. $1.07
d. $100

15. What is the value of the underlined digit in 23,085?

a. 8000
b. 800
c. 80
d. 8

16. Solve and place answer on the provided griddable sheet.

One number can correctly fill in all the blank boxes below. What is that number?

$$\_\_\_ \times 3 = 12$$
$$16 - \_\_\_ = 12$$
$$8 + \_\_\_ = 12$$

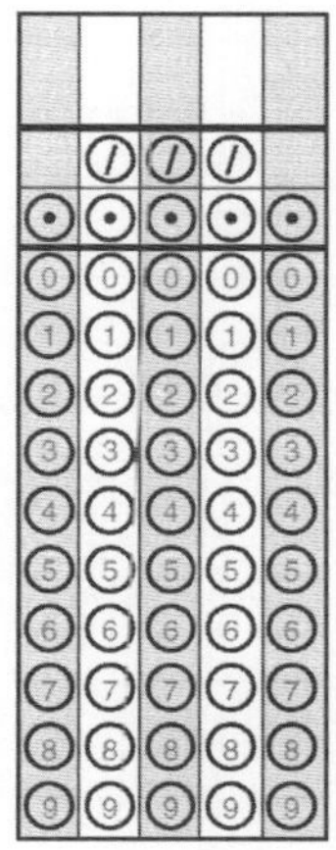

17. A class collects spiders. Spiders have 8 legs each. Which table shows the number of legs found on the spiders brought to class?

a.

Number of Spiders	Number of Legs
2	10
3	11
6	14
8	16
11	19

b.

Number of Spiders	Number of Legs
4	28
5	35
9	63
12	84
14	98

c.

Number of Spiders	Number of Legs
3	12
4	13
8	17
10	19
12	21

d.

Number of Spiders	Number of Legs
3	24
5	40
6	48
9	72
12	96

18. The total number of candy pieces found in different numbers of candy jars is shown in the table below.

Number of Candy Jars	Number of Candy Pieces
2	28
3	42
4	56
5	70

How many candy pieces are there in 8 candy jars?

a. 84
b. 126
c. 112
d. 98

19. Penny drinks 8 glasses of water each day. The number of glasses of water she drinks over a 7-day time span can be determined, using the number sentence: $8 \times 7 = ?$

Which number sentence would not show the number of glasses of water she drinks?

a. $? \div 8 = 7$
b. $7 \times 8 = ?$
c. $? \div 7 = 8$
d. $7 - 8 = ?$

20. Belinda draws a rectangle with a length of 6 cm. She draws a second rectangle with a length of 11 cm. Belinda continues drawing more rectangles, where for each rectangle drawn, she uses a length that is 5 more centimeters than the length of the previous rectangle. If this pattern continues, what will be the length of the 11th rectangle?

a. 46 cm
b. 54 cm
c. 56 cm
d. 61 cm

21. What is the next number in the sequence shown?

132, 123, 115, 108, 102

a. 82
b. 87
c. 92
d. 97

22. Which of the following figures is NOT congruent to the others shown?

a. 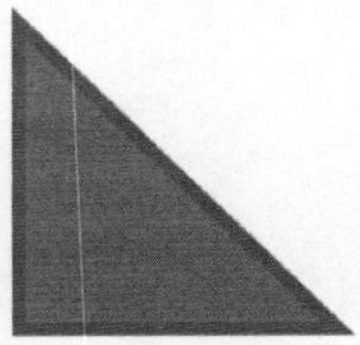

b. 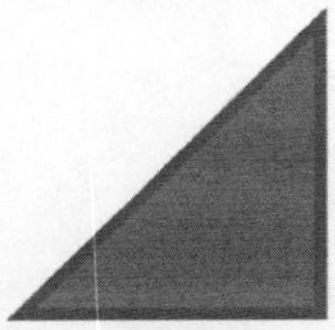

c. 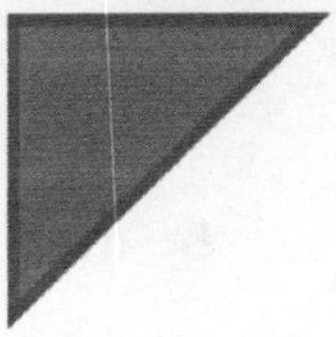

d. 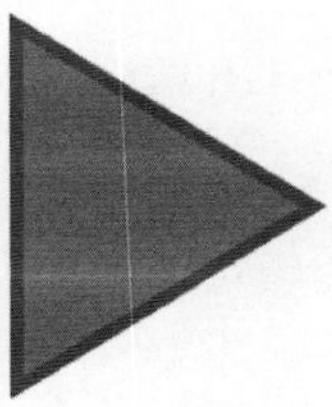

23. Which number is greater than the number shown by Point M on the number line?

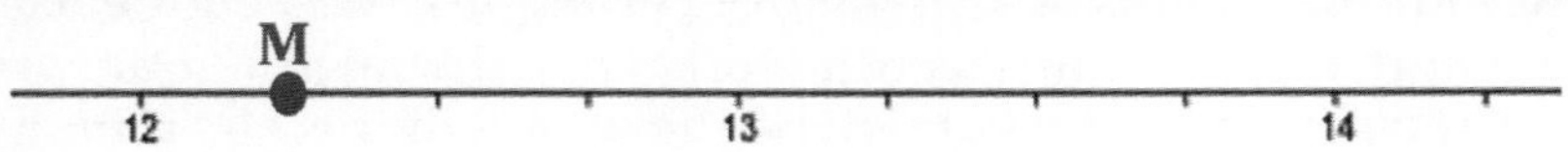

a. $12\frac{1}{4}$
b. $12\frac{1}{2}$
c. 12
d. $12\frac{3}{4}$

24. What is 788 rounded to the nearest ten?

a. 789
b. 800
c. 790
d. 780

25. Which of the following is true?

a. $\frac{3}{5} = \frac{4}{5}$
b. $\frac{3}{5} < \frac{4}{5}$
c. $\frac{2}{5} > \frac{4}{5}$
d. $\frac{2}{5} = \frac{4}{5}$

26. Which shape has the most sides?

a. Square
b. Triangle
c. Pentagon
d. Hexagon

27. In which place value is the digit 3 in 4,382?

a. Ones
b. Tens
c. Hundreds
d. Thousands

28. Find the sum of $\frac{12}{25} + \frac{7}{25}$.

a. $\frac{19}{50}$
b. $\frac{1}{5}$
c. $\frac{19}{25}$
d. $\frac{4}{5}$

29. What number does Point P represent?

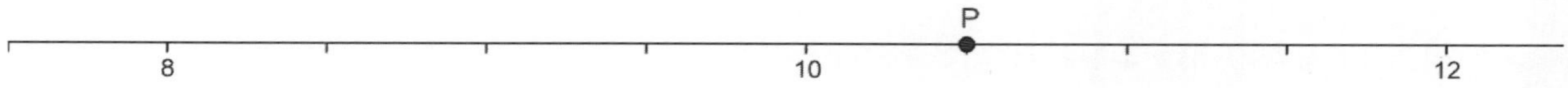

a. $10\frac{1}{4}$
b. $10\frac{1}{2}$
c. $10\frac{1}{3}$
d. $10\frac{3}{4}$

30. What is 125,420 rounded to the nearest hundred?

a. 400
b. 500
c. 125,000
d. 125,400

31. What is the perimeter of the triangle shown below?

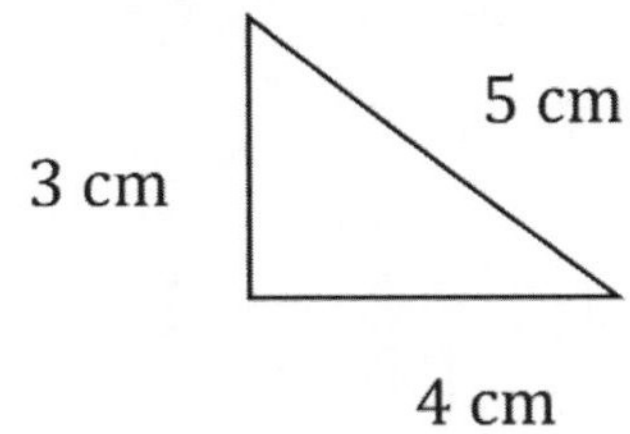

a. 6 cm
b. 12 cm
c. 9 cm
d. 8 cm

32. Which operation symbol properly compares $\frac{2}{3}$ and $\frac{5}{6}$?

a. >
b. =
c. <
d. Impossible to determine

33. Order these numbers from greatest to least.

4,586	7,324	9,126	3,854	4,789	9,087

a. 9,126; 7,324; 9,087; 4,568; 4,789; 3,854
b. 9,126; 9,087; 7,324; 4,789; 4,568; 3,854
c. 3,854; 4,568; 4,789; 7,324; 9,087; 9,126
d. 9,126; 9,087; 7,324; 4,568; 4,789; 3,854

34. A pencil is shown below. Use the ruler from your mathematics chart to measure the length of the pencil. About how long is the pencil, from base to tip, to the nearest inch?

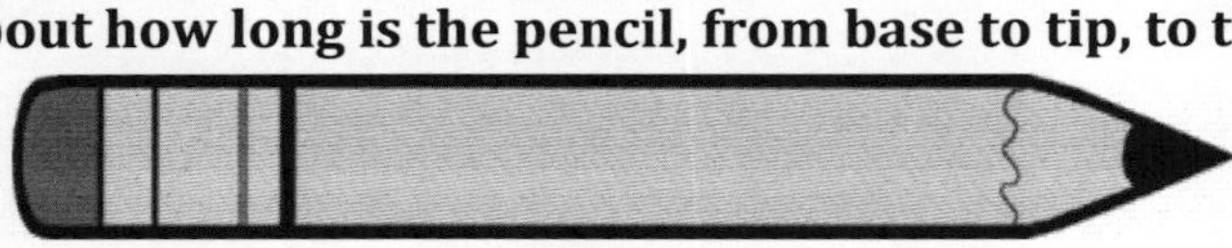

a. 2 in
b. 3 in
c. 4 in
d. 5 in

35. How many square units are found in the trapezoid below?

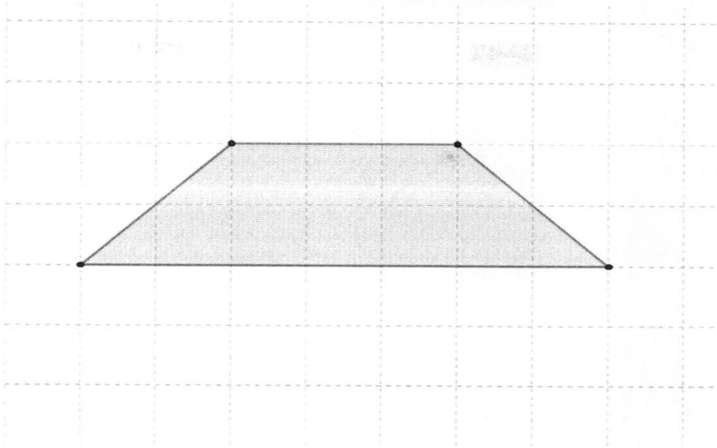

a. 8 square units
b. 12 square units
c. 10 square units
d. 9 square units

36.

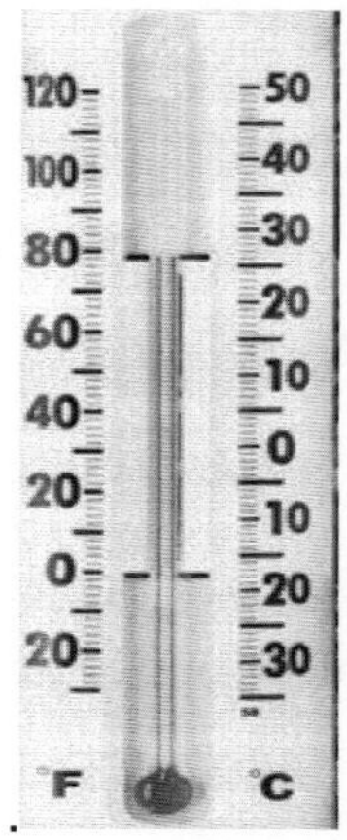

What is the approximate temperature, in degrees Fahrenheit?

a. 0° F
b. 80° F
c. 30° F
d. 25° F

37. Karen goes to the library at the time shown on the clock below. At what time does she go to the library?

a. 8:10
b. 1:30
c. 6:10
d. 2:30

38. Which clock below would be read as a five o'clock?

a. **5:00**

b. **5:30**

c. **5:05**

d. **5:55**

39. Aubrey rolls a die. Which of the following statements is true?

a. She is more likely to roll a 3 than a 6
b. She is equally likely to roll a 3 or a 6
c. She is less likely to roll a 3 than a 6
d. She is certain to roll a 3 or a 6

40. The bar graph below shows the number of zoos found in four states.

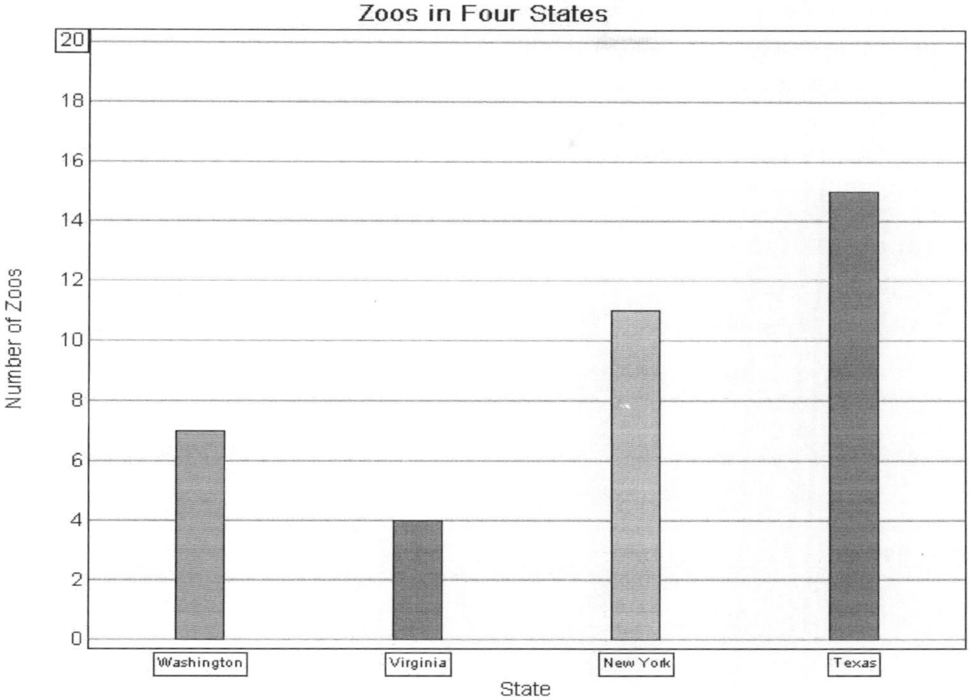

Which state has the most zoos?

a. Washington
b. Virginia
c. New York
d. Texas

41. A fish bowl contains 2 striped, 4 orange, and 2 blue fish. Eli randomly scoops a fish from the bowl. Which of the following statements is true?

a. He is less likely to scoop an orange than a striped fish
b. He is more likely to scoop a striped than a blue fish
c. He is more likely to scoop a blue than an orange fish
d. He is equally likely to scoop a striped and a blue fish

42. The number of lawns, finished by four different landscaping companies, in one week, is shown in the table below.

Landscaping Company	Number of Lawns
Landscaping Company A	12
Landscaping Company B	18
Landscaping Company C	6
Landscaping Company D	16

Which pictograph shows the number of lawns finished by each company?

a.
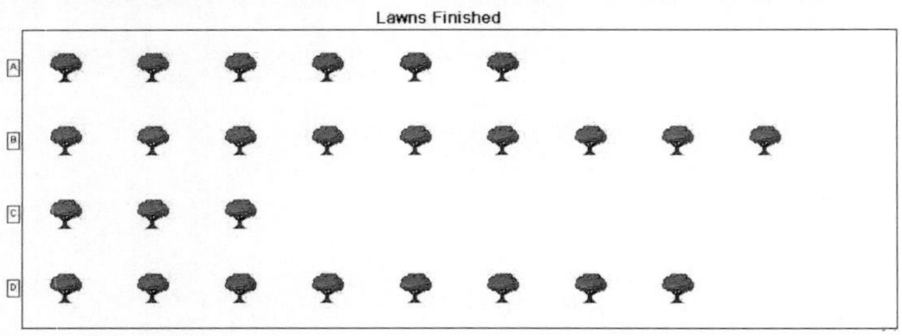

Each tree represents 2 lawns.

b.
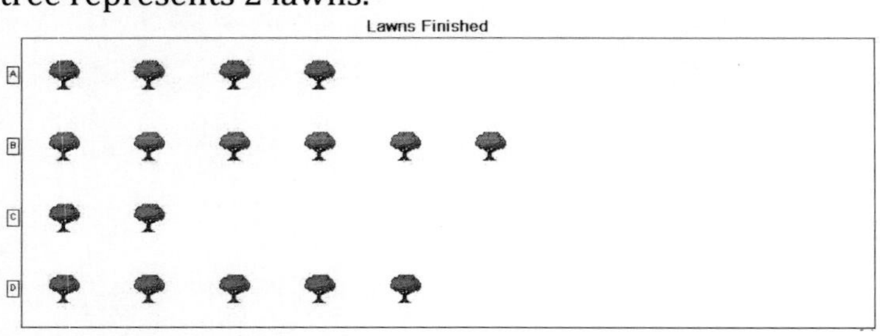

Each tree represents 4 lawns.

c.
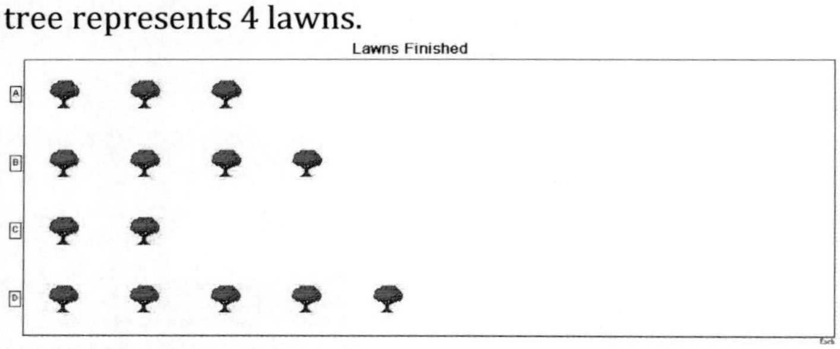

Each tree represents 2 lawns.

d.
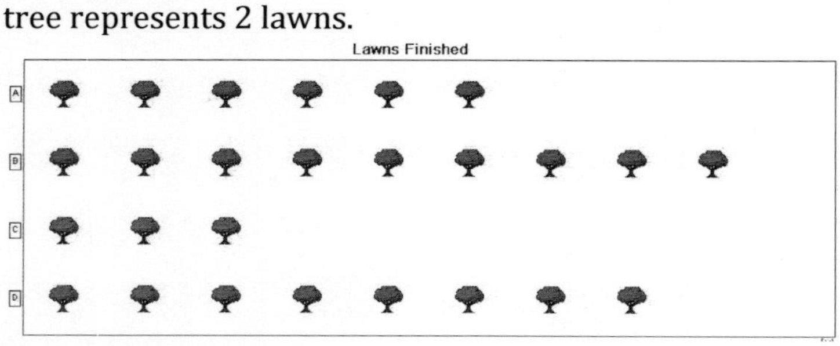

Each tree represents 3 lawns.

43. Which of the following events is certain?

a. Rolling a 7 on a die
b. Rolling an even number on a die
c. Rolling a number less than 8 on a die
d. Rolling an odd number on a die

44. The bar graph below shows the favorite sport of the students in the class.

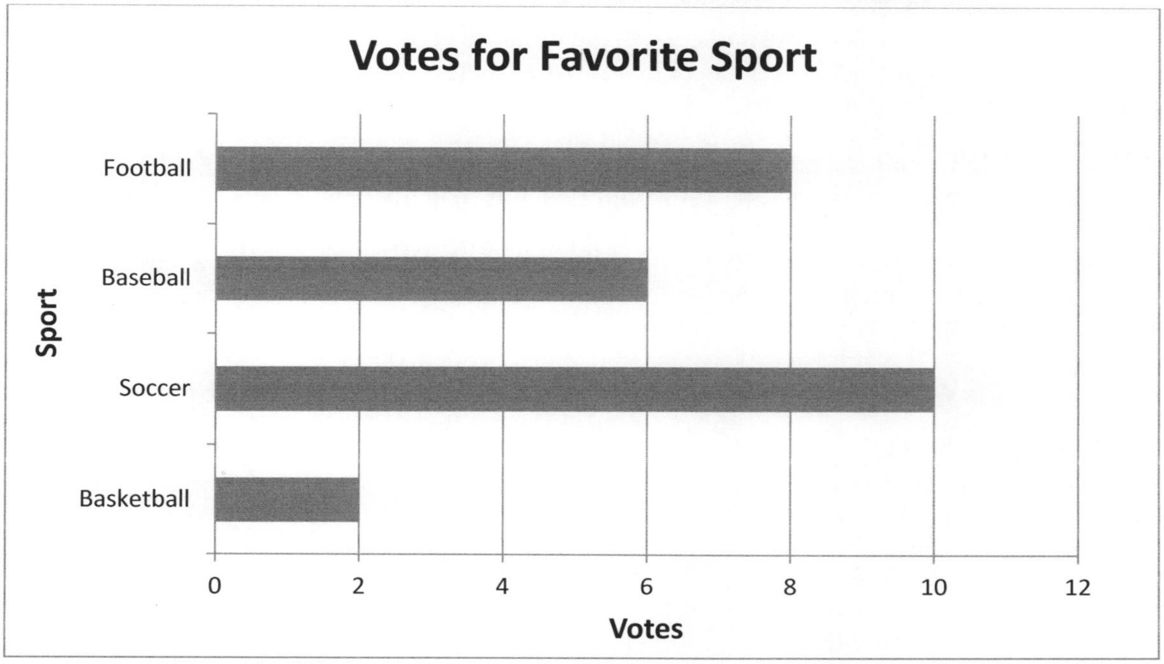

How many fewer votes did basketball get compared to baseball?

a. 2
b. 3
c. 4
d. 5

Answer Key and Explanations for Math Test #1

1. D: The annual expenses for Years 2009, 2007, 2008, 2011, and 2010 are $1,046, $1,224, $1,319, $1,342, and $1,529, respectively. These amounts are listed in order from lowest to highest. Since all of the numbers have a 1 in the thousands place, the numerals in the hundreds place must be compared. For the amounts of $1,319 and $1,342, the numerals in the tens place must be compared. No other choice shows the years listed in increasing order of expense.

2. C: There are 2 dollar bills, which represent 2 dollars. There are also 2 quarters, 2 nickels, 1 dime, and 4 pennies. Two quarters are worth $0.50 since each is worth $0.25 $(2 \times 0.25 = 0.50)$, 2 nickels are worth $0.10 since each is worth $0.05 $(2 \times 0.05 = 0.10)$, 1 dime is worth $0.10, and 4 pennies are worth $0.04 since each is worth $0.01. The sum of the coins can be found by writing: $0.50 + $0.10 + $0.10 + $0.04, which equals $0.74. The sum of the two dollar bills and the coins can be written as: $2.00 + $0.74. Thus, he paid $2.74.

3. B: If $\frac{1}{3}$ of the balls Wyatt received were basketballs that means the remaining balls he received must have been soccer balls. Since the fraction used is $\frac{1}{3}$, look at it as if he received 3 balls. One ball was a basketball and the remaining balls had to be soccer balls. This is now a simple subtraction problem. $3 - 1 = 2$ soccer balls.

4. D: The numbers: 608, 458, 452, 381, 321, and 294 are written in order from greatest to least. An examination of the numerals in the hundreds place reveals that 608 is the greatest and 294 is the least. The numbers, 458 and 452, are greater than the numbers, 381 and 321, based on the value of the digits in the hundreds place. An examination of the numerals in the ones place, since both the digits in the hundreds and the tens places are the same, allows you to compare 458 and 452, which shows 458 to be the larger number. An examination of the numerals in the tens place allows you to compare 381 and 321, since the digits in the hundreds place are the same, which shows 381 to be the larger number. None of the other choices show the numbers in descending order.

5. C: Choice C shows 2 triangles and 4 hexagons, which is a total of 6 shapes. The fraction 2 out of 6, or $\frac{2}{6}$, also represents 1 out of 3, or $\frac{1}{3}$. None of the other choices represent this fraction: Choice A shows $\frac{3}{6}$, which equals $\frac{1}{2}$. Choice B shows $\frac{1}{4}$. Choice D shows $\frac{1}{6}$.

6. C: The diagram shows 32 counters divided into 4 groups, with 8 counters in each group. Therefore, the total number of counters, 32, is divided by 4, giving a quotient of 8, which is written as: $32 \div 4 = 8$.

7. 480: This is a simple multiplication problem which involves carrying the excess (greater than a single digit) to the next column. Start with the 5 and multiply each digit above: $5 \times 6 = 30$. Write down the 0 and place the 3 on top of the 9. Multiply 5×9 to get 45. Add in the 3 to get 48. Write down the number 48 and the product is 480.

8. D: The total number of feet he ascended can be determined by adding 482 feet and 362 feet. The sum of 482 and 362 is 844. Thus, he ascended 844 feet in all.

9. B: The item priced at \$62 can be rounded to \$60. The item priced at \$89 can be rounded to \$90. The sum of 60 and 90 is 150. Thus, the best estimate is \$150.

10. B: Choice B shows 4 shaded sections out of 6 total sections. The fraction, $\frac{4}{6}$, is the same as the fraction, $\frac{2}{3}$. Two shaded sections represent one-third of the total. Thus, four shaded sections represent two-thirds of the total. Each of the pictures has 6 total sections, so the other choices can be written as fractions with a 6 in the denominator. Choice A shows $\frac{3}{6}$, which equals $\frac{1}{2}$. Choice C shows . Choice D shows $\frac{2}{6}$, which equals $\frac{1}{3}$. So, only Choice B shows the correct picture.

11. D: A possible first step would be to divide the number of tiles glued each day by the number of hours it took to glue the tiles. The two quotients would then represent approximately how many tiles glued per hour, and could then be compared.

12. 50: Begin with the tokens given to each guest, which was 12. But the problem states that every game takes two tokens, so each guest can play only 6 games, not 12. Multiply this by the number of guests, 9, to equal 54 games. Round this number to the nearest tens to get 50.

13. C: Each number is 8 more than the previous number, which means that the next number can be found by adding 8 to the previous number. Thus, the fifth number is 353, the sixth number is 361, the seventh number is 369, and the eighth number is 377.

14. C: Convert the coins to cents and apply addition. Each nickel is worth 5 cents, so 3 nickels equals 15 cents. Each dime is worth 10 cents, so 4 dimes equals 40 cents. Each penny is worth 1 cent, so 2 pennies equals 2 cents. A quarter is worth 25 cents, so 2 quarters equals 50 cents. $15 + 40 + 2 + 50 = 107$ cents. Since there are 100 cents in a dollar, this becomes 1 dollar with 7 cents remaining or \$1.07

15. C: The place value is assigned by the position of the digit. The places from left to right are ones, tens, hundreds, thousands, ten-thousands, etc. Since the digit 8 is in the second place from the left, it is in the tens place. The value of the digit is 8×10, which is 80.

16. 12: The correct answer is 4. $4 \times 3 = 12$; $16 - 4 = 12$, and $8 + 4 = 12$.

17. D: Each spider has 8 legs. In order to find the number of legs present with 3 spiders, you multiply 3 by 8, which is 24. Thus, 3 spiders have 24 legs in all. Choice D is the only table that shows each number of spiders, multiplied by 8, to yield the correct product representing the total number of legs.

18. C: Each candy jar has 14 pieces of candy. This can be determined by dividing the number of pieces of candy by the number of candy jars: $28 \div 2 = 14, 42 \div 3 = 14, 56 \div 4 = 14, 70 \div 5 = 14$. Since the data in the table shows that there are 14 pieces of candy in each jar, multiplying $8 \times 14 = 112$ finds the total number of pieces of candy that are in 8 candy jars.

19. D: If she drinks 8 glasses of water each day, the number of glasses of water she drinks in 12 days can be determined by multiplying 8 by 7. This product is 56; thus she drinks 56 glasses of water in a 7-day time span. The relationship between the number of glasses of water she drinks per day and the total number of glasses of water she drinks in 7 days can be represented by an appropriate multiplication or division number sentence within the following fact family: $8 \times 7 = 56, 56 \div 8 = 7, 7 \times 8 = 56, 56 \div 7 = 8$. Subtracting 8 from 7 will not reveal the number of glasses she drinks in a 7-day time span. The number sentence: $7 - 8 = ?$, is not in this fact family.

20. C: If each rectangle has a length that is 5 cm more than that of the previous rectangle, the lengths of the 3rd rectangle through the 11th rectangle can be found by adding 5 cm to the length of the second triangle and continuing for each next rectangle. So, the lengths of the rectangles will be as follows: 16 cm, 21 cm, 26 cm, 31 cm, 36 cm, 41 cm, 46 cm, 51 cm, and 56 cm.

21. D: The pattern is subtracting one less number each time:

$$132 - 9 = 123$$
$$123 - 8 = 115$$
$$115 - 7 = 108$$
$$108 - 6 = 102$$

The next number to be subtracted is 5, so $102 - 5 = 97$.

22. D: Choices A, B, and C are all the same right triangle just flipped around. Answer choice D is a different triangle and therefore not congruent.

23. D: $12\frac{1}{4}$ is represented by the first tick mark to the right of the 12. $12\frac{1}{2}$ is the second tick mark and $12\frac{3}{4}$ is the third tick mark, or the tick mark before the 13. Only $12\frac{3}{4}$ appears to the right of point M on the number line, making it greater.

24. C: The place value of a digit depends on its location in relation to the decimal point. The places to the left of the decimal are ones, tens, then hundreds, respectively. To round a number to a certain place value, look at the digit to the immediate right. If the digit to the right is 5 or more, round up by adding one. If the digit is less than five, round down by keeping the same digit. For this problem, the digit in the tens place is 8. The digit to its immediate right is 8. Since 8 is greater than 5, round up: 788 rounded to the nearest ten is 790.

25. B: $\frac{3}{5}$ is less than $\frac{4}{5}$. They are not equal. When comparing fractions with the same denominator, compare only the values in the numerator. Since they share a common denominator of 5, compare only the 3 and 4. Since 3 is less than 4, the same can be said for the fraction $\frac{3}{5}$ when compared to $\frac{4}{5}$.

26. D: A hexagon has 6 sides. A square has 4 sides. A triangle has 3 sides. A pentagon has 5 sides. Therefore, a hexagon has the most number of sides out of the options provided.

27. C: The place value is assigned by the position of the digit. The places from left to right are ones, tens, hundreds, thousands, ten-thousands, etc. The 3 is located in the hundreds place since it is three spaces from the left.

28. C: When adding fractions together that share a common denominator, add the numerators together and leave the denominator the same. Since both fractions share a denominator of 25, the numerators can be added together. 12 plus 7 is equal to 19. Therefore, $\frac{12}{25} + \frac{7}{25} = \mathbf{\frac{19}{25}}$.

29. B: Each increment represents one-half. This can be determined by counting that there are 3 marks, or 4 spaces, that lie between the difference of two wholes, as in between 10 and 12. Thus, one increment past 10, where Point P is located, represents $10\frac{1}{2}$.

30. D: The place value of a digit depends on its location in relation to the decimal point. The places to the left of the decimal are ones, tens, then hundreds, respectively. To round a number to a certain place value, look at the digit to the immediate right. If the digit to the right is 5 or more, round up by adding one followed by a zero. If the digit is less than five, round down by keeping the same digit followed by a zero. For this problem, the digit in the hundreds place is 4. The digit to its immediate right is 2. Since 2 is less than 5, round down. So, 125,420 rounded to the nearest hundred is 125,400.

31. B: The distance around the triangle, or the perimeter, is equal to the sum of 3 cm, 5 cm, and 4 cm. Thus, the perimeter is 12 cm.

32. C: One way to compare two fractions is by making two strip diagrams. The denominator represents how many equal spaces the strip will be divided into. The numerator represents how many spaces on the strip will be shaded in. It is important to make the strip diagrams the same size to accurately compare the fractions. When looking at the strip diagrams, it is evident that $\frac{2}{3}$ is less than $\frac{5}{6}$.

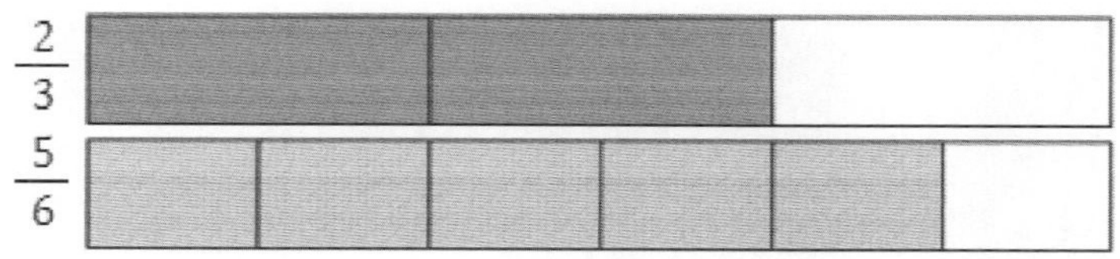

33. B: The correct order when order from greatest to least is 9,126; 9,087; 7,324; 4,789; 4,568; 3,854. 9,126 is the furthest to the right on the number line, so it is the largest. 3,854 is the furthest to the left on the number line, so it is the smallest.

34. B: The pencil is approximately 3.25 inches, which rounds to 3 inches.

35. C: The trapezoid has 8 square units, plus 4 one-half square units, which equals 2 more square units. The sum of 8 square units and 2 square units is 10 square units.

36. B: The thermometer shows the temperature to be very close to 80 degrees Fahrenheit. It also shows the temperature in Celsius: about 25 degrees.

37. C: The short hand, or hour hand, is between 6 o'clock and 7 o'clock, revealing that Karen went to the library after 6 o'clock. The long hand, or minute hand, is pointed at the 2. Since the 2 on the clock represents 10 minutes after the hour (since each number shown on the clock represents 5 minutes and $2 \times 5 = 10$), the clock shows that Karen went to the library at 6:10.

38. A: Five o'clock shown on a digital clock would be shown as a 5 followed by two zeroes, indicating no minutes.

39. B: Since a die has one of each number, from 1 to 6, she is equally likely to roll any of the six numbers. The possibility of rolling one of these numbers is no more or less than the possibility of rolling another of these numbers. Thus, she is equally likely to roll a 3 or a 6.

40. D: Texas has the most zoos because it has 15 zoos, while the other states each have 7 zoos, 4 zoos, and 11 zoos. Also, it can be seen from the graph that the bar representing Texas is much higher than the bars for the other states.

41. D: The more fish there is of a certain color the more likely it is that the color of fish is scooped. With more orange fish than striped fish in the bowl, he is more likely to scoop an orange fish than a striped one. There are equal amounts of striped and blue fish, so one is not more likely than the other. There are more orange fish than blue fish, so he is more likely to scoop an orange fish than a blue one.. Finally, the number of striped and blue fish is the same – so they are equally likely to be scooped compared to each other. Thus, Choice D is the only true statement.

42. A: Since each tree represents 2 lawns, the pictograph shows that the number of lawns finished by Company A is equal to 6×2, or 12 lawns, the number of lawns finished by Company B is equal to 9×2, or 18 lawns, the number of lawns finished by Company C is equal to 3×2, or 6 lawns, and the number of lawns finished by Company D is equal to 8×2, or 16 lawns. This is the only pictograph that represents the correct number of lawns.

43. C: A die has numbers 1-6, so rolling a number less than 8 is a certain occurrence. It will always happen. Choice A is incorrect because rolling a 7 would be impossible. Choices B and D are also incorrect because rolling either an even or odd number, since the die has both, would not be certain.

44. C: Baseball received 6 votes and basketball received only 2 votes. The difference is $6 - 2 = 4$ fewer votes.

Math Practice Test #2

1. What is the value of the underlined digit in $4\underline{5},162$?

a. 5000
b. 500
c. 50
d. 5

2. Which numbers are listed in order from least to greatest?

a. 539, 542, 528, 576, 588
b. 588, 576, 542, 539, 528
c. 528, 542, 539, 588, 576
d. 528, 539, 542, 576, 588

3. Which of the following is equations represents five subtracted from twenty-five equals twenty?

a. $25 - 20 = 5$
b. $5 - 25 = 5$
c. $25 - 5 = 20$
d. $20 + 5 = 25$

4. Camille's teacher passed out crayons and pencils to students in her class. One-fourth of the writing tools Camille received were crayons. Which of the following could represent the number of crayons she received?

a. 

b. 

c. 

d. 

5. Bercu sells 128 hot dogs this month. She sold 117 hot dogs last month. How many hot dogs has she sold in these past two months?

a. 235
b. 241
c. 242
d. 245

6. Chandler paid for a book at a book fare. He gave the clerk the amount of money shown below. How much money did he give the clerk?

a. $2.57
b. $2.72
c. $2.77
d. $2.82

7. What number sentence is shown by the diagram below?

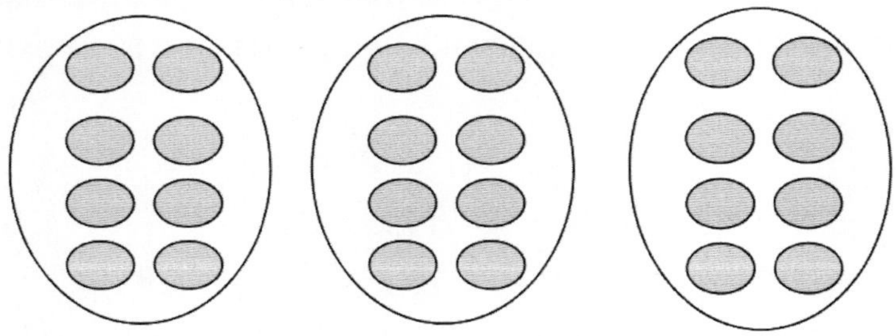

a. $24 \times 3 = 72$
b. $24 - 8 = 16$
c. $24 + 8 = 32$
d. $24 \div 3 = 8$

8. Solve and place answer on the provided griddable sheet.

$$\begin{array}{r} 78 \\ \underline{\times\ 4} \end{array}$$

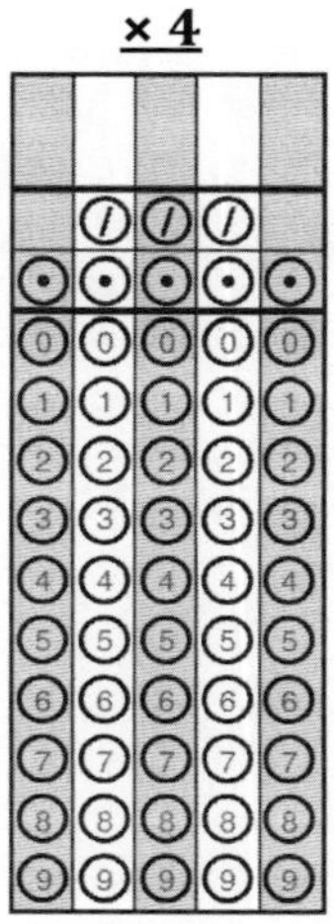

9. On Monday morning, a store manager gave 3 coupons to every customer who entered the store. If 89 people entered the store that morning, which is the best estimate for the total number of coupons the store manager gave to customers?

a. 300
b. 270
c. 480
d. 180

10. Farm A has 8 chickens and 3 horses. Farm B has 6 chickens and 5 horses. Which of the following is a possible first step in determining which farm contains more animal feet?

a. Multiply the number of chickens on each farm by 2, and multiply the number of horses on each farm by 4
b. Find the total number of animals found on both farms
c. Multiply the sum of the number of chickens and horses, found on both farms, by 6
d. Add 2 to the number of chickens found on each farm, and add 4 to the number of horses found on each farm

11. Which model shows a fraction that is more than 4 out of 7?

a. 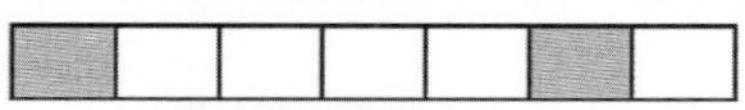
b. 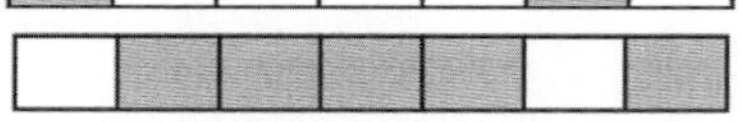
c. 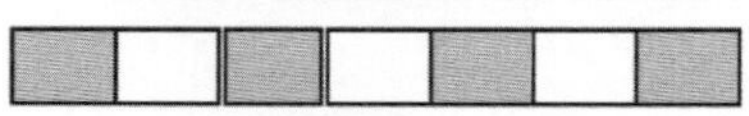
d. 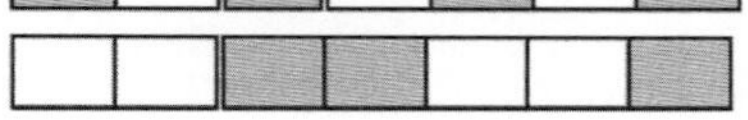

12. The number of miles Jacob has walked each year over the past five years is shown in the table below.

Year 1	691
Year 2	567
Year 3	144
Year 4	963
Year 5	221

Which sequence of years shows the number of miles he walked each year, listed in order from greatest to least?

a. Year 2, Year 4, Year 5, Year 1, Year 3
b. Year 4, Year 1, Year 2, Year 5, Year 3
c. Year 1, Year 4, Year 2, Year 5, Year 3
d. Year 3, Year 2, Year 5, Year 4, Year 1

13. A neighborhood contains 3 streets. Street 1 has 26 houses, Street 2 has 12 houses, and Street 3 has 35 houses. Estimate by rounding, how many houses in total are on Street 1 and Street 3?

a. 30
b. 40
c. 50
d. 60

14. A little girl has two nickels, two dimes, four pennies, and one quarter. How much money does she have?

a. 30 cents
b. 90 cents
c. 60 cents
d. 40 cents

15. What is the seventh number in the pattern below?

228, 235, 242, 249, ___, ___, ___

a. 269
b. 256
c. 270
d. 263

16. A farmer plants rows of corn each growing season. The table below shows the total number of rows of corn the farmer has planted after several seasons.

Season	Number of Rows
Season 2	34
Season 4	68
Season 6	102
Season 8	136
Season 10	

How many rows of corn will the farmer have planted by the end of Season 10?

a. 153
b. 170
c. 136
d. 168

17. In which place value is the digit 4 in 7,843?

a. Ones
b. Tens
c. Hundreds
d. Thousands

18. Anand has 45 stamps in his collection. He decides to give all of his stamps to 5 friends. He writes the number sentence below to find out how many stamps to give each friend, if each friend is to receive an equal amount.

$$45 \div 5 = ?$$

Which number sentence would NOT help him find the number of stamps to give each friend?

a. $? \times 5 = 45$
b. $45 - 5 = ?$
c. $45 \div ? = 5$
d. $5 \times ? = 45$

19. What is the next item in the pattern below?

a. 

b. 

c. 

d. 

20. Hannah builds the towers shown below, using square blocks.

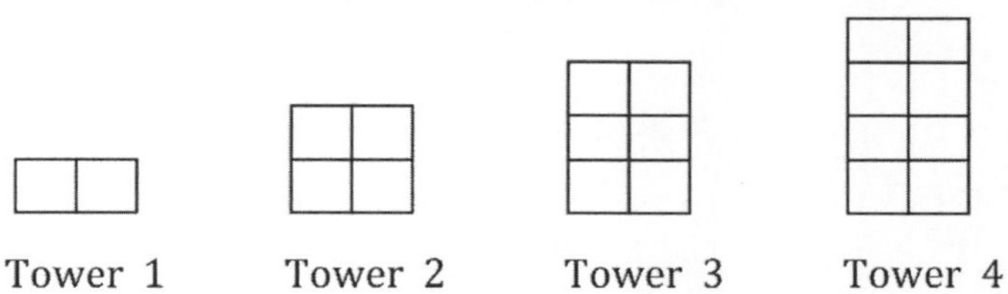

If she continues this pattern, how many square blocks will she use in the eighth tower?

a. 12
b. 16
c. 18
d. 14

21. The table below shows the number of books students brought to share with the class.

Number of Students	Number of Books
2	8
5	20
6	24
8	32

How many books did 12 students bring?

a. 44
b. 36
c. 40
d. 48

22. Jordan wants to show the number of wheels found on several cars. Which table should he use?

a.

Number of Cars	Number of Wheels
3	12
4	16
7	28
11	44
12	48

b.

Number of Cars	Number of Wheels
2	6
5	15
8	24
9	27
12	36

c.

Number of Cars	Number of Wheels
3	15
5	25
6	30
8	40
11	55

d.

Number of Cars	Number of Wheels
4	8
6	12
9	18
12	24
14	28

23. What is 49,249 rounded to the nearest hundred?

a. 49,200
b. 200
c. 49,250
d. 49,300

24. Which operation symbol properly compares $\frac{1}{3}$ and $\frac{11}{12}$?

a. <
b. =
c. >
d. Impossible to determine

25. Which number is greater than the number shown by Point S on the number line?

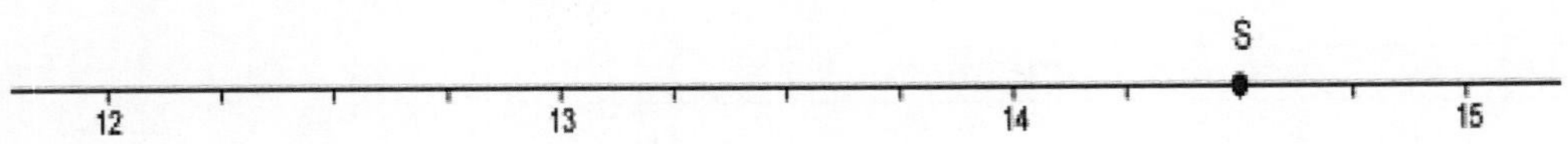

a. $14\frac{1}{4}$
b. 14
c. $14\frac{3}{4}$
d. $14\frac{1}{2}$

26. Which of the following values lies between $\frac{3}{14}$ and $\frac{7}{14}$?

a. $\frac{1}{14}$
b. $\frac{3}{14}$
c. $\frac{9}{14}$
d. $\frac{6}{14}$

27. Which of the following is congruent to the triangle shown below?

a.  c. 

b. 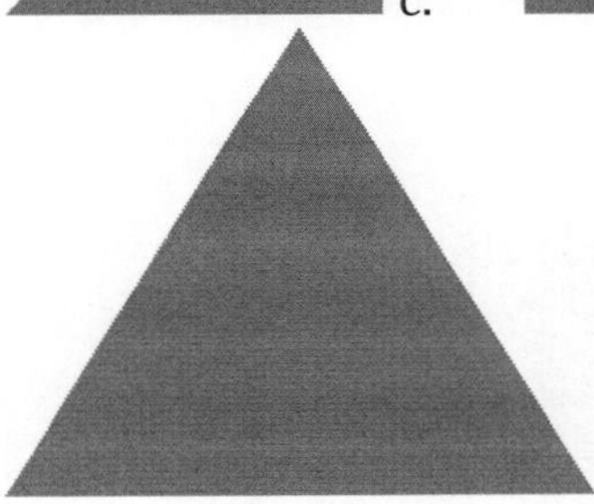 d. 

28. Which of the following figures has fewer than 6 sides?

a. Pentagon
b. Octagon
c. Nonagon
d. Decagon

29. What is 6,709 rounded to the nearest ten?

a. 6,700
b. 6,710
c. 7,000
d. 6,810

30. Ashley states, "All two-dimensional shapes are polygons." Which of the following shapes proves this statement to be false?

a. Triangles
b. Rectangles
c. Circles
d. Hexagons

31. What is the perimeter of the shape shown below?

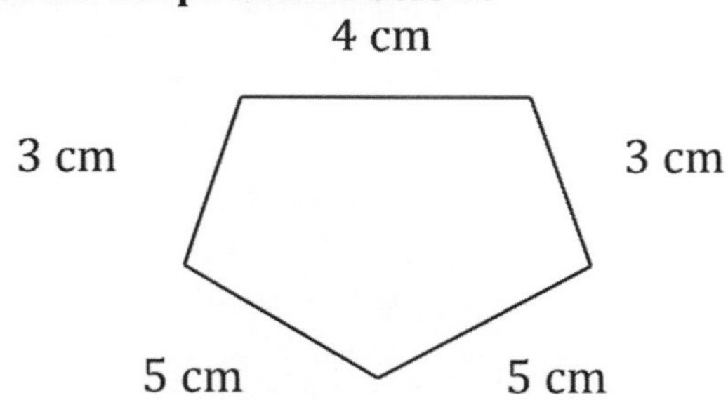

a. 29 cm
b. 20 cm
c. 15 cm
d. 25 cm

32. Which of the following is true?

a. $\frac{7}{12} = \frac{9}{12}$
b. $\frac{9}{12} < \frac{9}{12}$
c. $\frac{9}{12} > \frac{7}{12}$
d. $\frac{9}{12} = \frac{7}{12}$

33. About how wide is the drawing of the notebook shown below?

a. 2 cm
b. 3 cm
c. 5 cm
d. 7 cm

34. How many square units are found in the shape below?

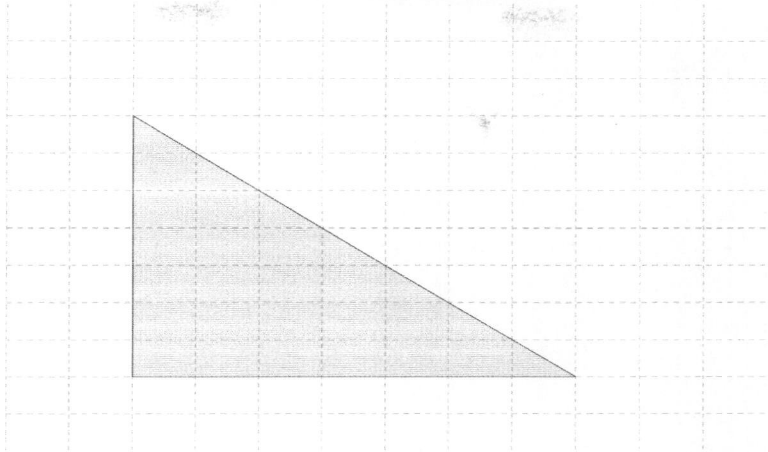

a. 23 square units
b. $23\frac{1}{2}$ square units
c. 24 square units
d. $24\frac{1}{2}$ square units

35. Which operation symbol properly compares $\frac{2}{4}$ and $\frac{5}{10}$?

a. <
b. =
c. >
d. Impossible to determine

36. The outside temperature, on a spring day, in Flagstaff, Arizona, is shown on the thermometer below.

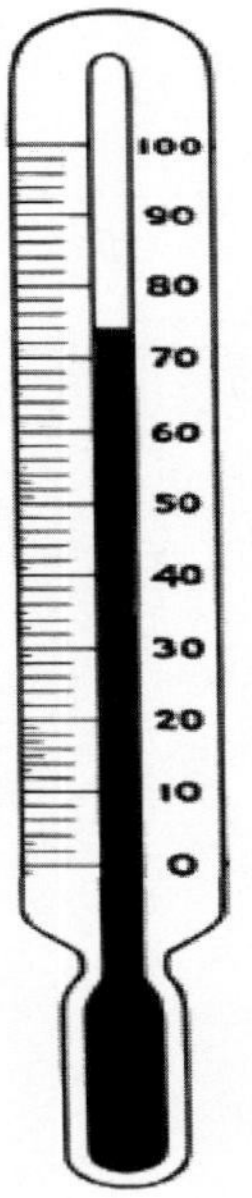

What is the temperature, in degrees Fahrenheit?

a. 77° F
b. 76° F
c. 79° F
d. 74° F

37. Amanda arrives at a birthday party at the time shown on the clock below.

What time did she arrive at the party?

a. 10:10
b. 2:10
c. 9:10
d. 2:50

38. Which clock below would be read as a quarter past three?

a.

3:25

b.

3:15

c.

3:45

d.

3:30

39. A bag contains 3 red cards, 7 blue cards, 9 green cards, and 6 yellow cards. Jesse randomly draws a card from the bag. Which of the following statements is true?

a. He is less likely to draw a green card than a yellow card
b. He is more likely to draw a yellow card than a red card
c. He is more likely to draw a yellow card than a blue card
d. He is equally likely to draw a red, blue, green, or yellow card

40. The number of cakes baked in one month, by different bakeries, is shown in the table below.

Bakery	Bakery A	Bakery B	Bakery C	Bakery D
Number of Cakes Baked	25	15	35	20

Which pictograph shows the number of cakes baked by each bakery?

a. Each picture of a cake represents 5 cakes.

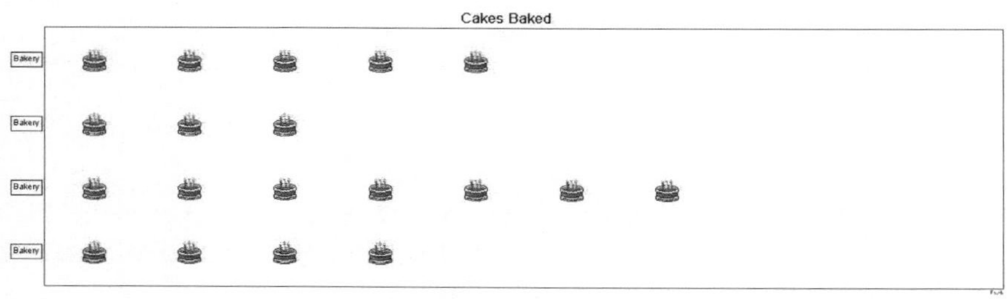

b. Each picture of a cake represents 4 cakes.

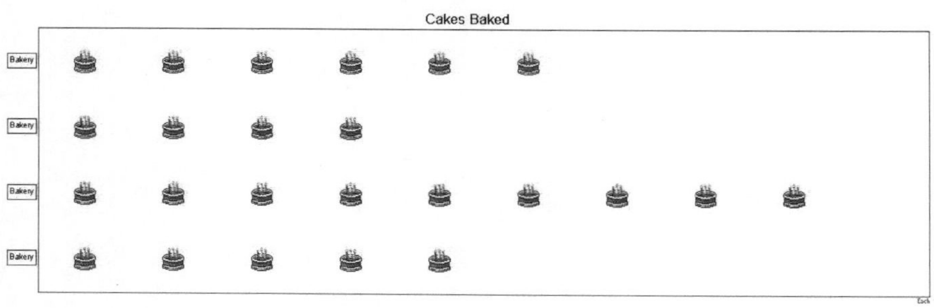

c. Each picture of a cake represents 3 cakes.

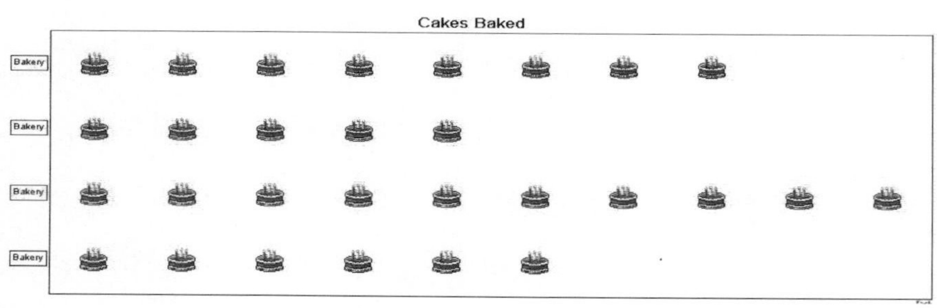

d. Each picture of a cake represents 6 cakes.

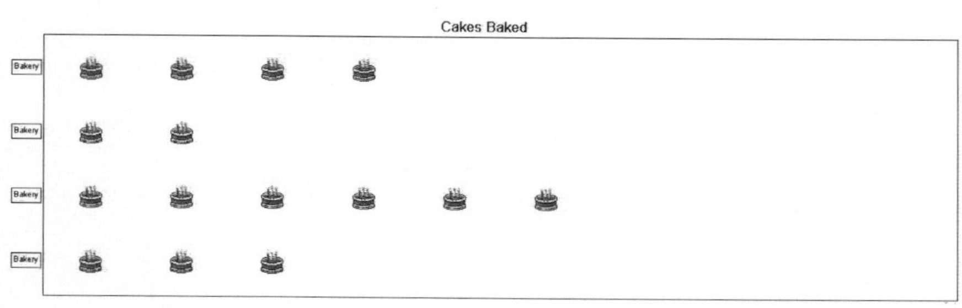

41. The bar graph below shows the number of Math teachers, from four different states, attending a math event.

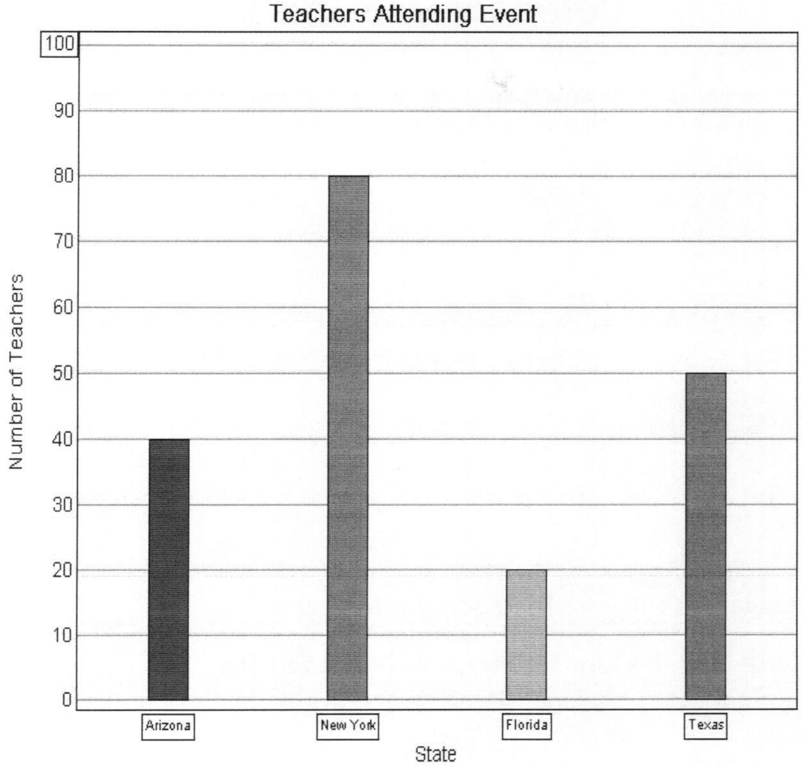

Which state has the fewest number of teachers attending the math event?

a. Arizona
b. New York
c. Florida
d. Texas

42. A student spins a spinner, with sections, labeled 1 – 8. Which of the following best represents the likelihood of the spinner landing on a 9?

a. Likely
b. Not likely
c. Certain
d. Impossible

43. Order these numbers from greatest to least.

591	602	592	573	584	588

a. 602; 592; 591; 584; 588; 573
b. 602; 591; 592; 588; 584; 573
c. 573; 584; 588; 591; 592; 602
d. 602; 592; 591; 588; 584; 573

44. The bar graph below shows the number of votes for choosing a class mascot.

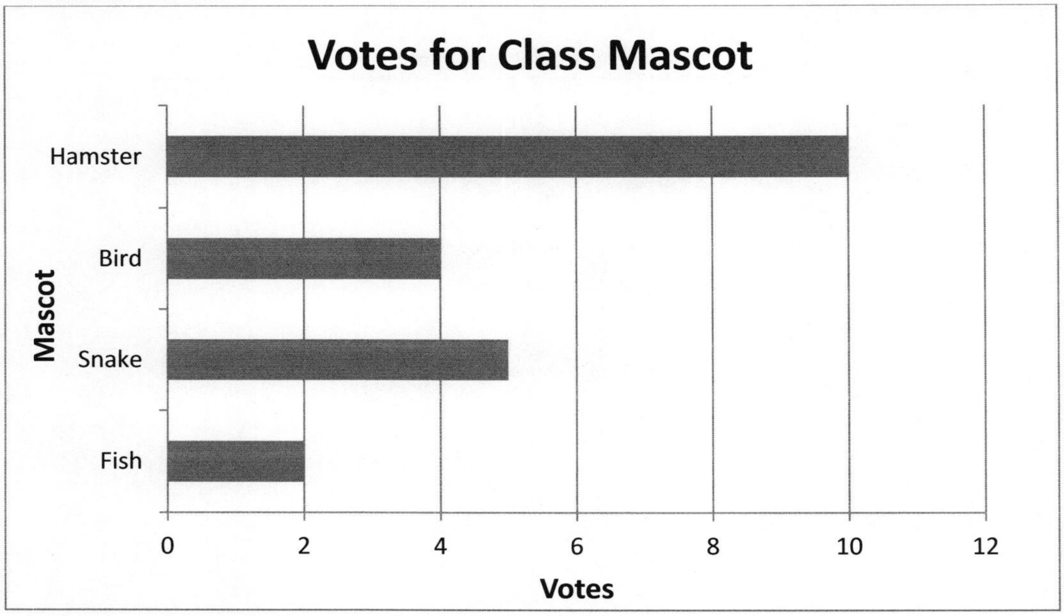

Solve and place answer on the provided griddable sheet.

How many more votes did the hamster receive than the fish?

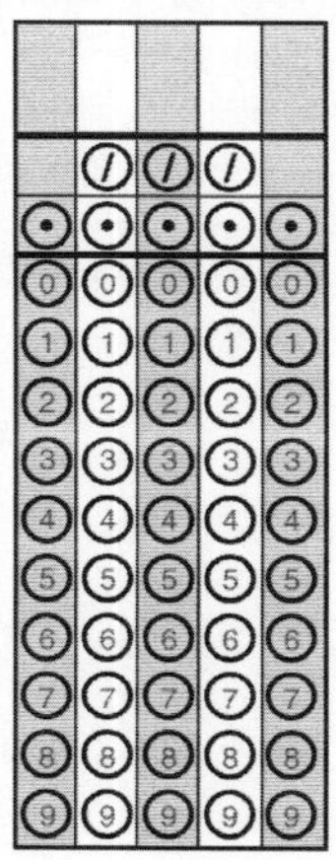

Answer Key and Explanations for Math Test #2

1. A: The place value is assigned by the position of the digit. The places from left to right are ones, tens, hundreds, thousands, ten-thousands, etc. Since the digit 5 is in the fourth place from the left, it is in the thousands place. The value of the digit is 5×1000, which is 5000.

2. D: All numbers for Choice D have a 5 in the hundreds place, indicating that the next digit, in the tens place, must be used to make comparisons. Each digit in the tens place is different, so an examination of the ones place is not needed. The list of increasing tens place digits for Choice D are 2, 3, 4, 7, and 8, indicating a correct ordering of the numbers from least to greatest. None of the other choices show strictly increasing numbers.

3. C: The term subtracted from means to "take away" and place a minus sign in the equation. Since 5 is being subtracted from 25, write the number 25 first followed by a minus sign and then the number 5. The problem states that this subtraction equals 5, so simply attach this to the end.

4. D: Choice D shows 1 crayon and 3 pencils, indicating that 1 out of 4 of Camille's writing tools were crayons. The other choices are out of either a total of 7 writing tools or 5 writing tools, which cannot be used in a ratio that represents 1 out of 4.

5. D: In order to find out the total number of hot dogs she sold in the two months, the amount sold in each month should be added. The sum of 128 and 117 is 245. Thus, she sold 245 hot dogs during the two months.

6. D: Two dollar bills are worth \$2.00. A quarter is worth \$0.25, 4 dimes are worth \$0.40 since they are worth \$0.10 each $(4 \times 0.10 = 0.40)$, 3 nickels are worth \$0.15 since they are worth \$0.05 each $(3 \times 0.05 = 0.15)$, and 2 pennies are worth \$0.02 since each is worth \$0.01. The sum of the coins is: $\$0.25 + \$0.40 + \$0.15 + \$0.02$, which equals \$0.82. The sum of the two dollar bills and the coins can be written as: $\$2.00 + \$0.82$, which equals \$2.82.

7. D: The diagram shows 24 counters total, divided into 3 groups, with 8 counters in each group. Therefore, the total number of counters, 24, is divided by 3. This gives a quotient of 8, which is written as: $24 \div 3 = 8$.

8. 312: This is a simple multiplication problem which involves carrying the excess (greater than a single digit) to the next column. Start with the 4 and multiply each digit above: $4 \times 8 = 32$. Write down the 2 and place the 3 on top of the 7. Multiply $4 \times 7$to get 28. Add in the 3 to get 31. Write down the number 31 and the product is 312.

9. B: The number of customers who entered the store can be rounded to 90. That number can be multiplied by 3, since each customer receives 6 coupons. The product of 90×3 is 270.

10. A: Since a chicken has 2 feet and a horse has 4 feet, you may multiply the number of chickens found on each farm by 2, and then multiply the number of horses found on each farm by 4. After finding the total number of chicken feet and horse feet on each farm, you can then add the two amounts to find the total number of animal feet on each farm. You can then compare the two values to determine the one that is larger.

11. B: Each model shows a whole, split into 7 sections. This makes the denominator equal to 7 for the fraction representing the shaded section for each. Since the fractions all have the same number on the bottom, the number of shaded sections can be compared. For a fraction to be more than $\frac{4}{7}$, more than 4 parts must be shaded. The model shown for Choice B shows the fraction $\frac{6}{7}$, because 6 out of 7 sections are shaded, showing a fraction that is more than 4 out of 7. The other choices all show either 4 parts or less than 4 parts shaded.

12. B: The sequence of the number of miles walked in order from greatest to least is: 963 (Year 4), 691 (Year 1), 567 (Year 2), 221 (Year 5), 144 (Year 3). The number of miles walked can also be compared by examining only the digits in the hundreds place since they are all different. 9 is greater than 6 which is greater than 5 and so on. The only choice that shows the years for the number of miles walked in descending order is B.

13. D: $26 + 35 = 61$. Since the 1 in the ones digit is less than five, the number is rounded down to 60.

14. C: Convert the coins to cents and apply addition. Each nickel is worth 5 cents, so 2 nickels equals 10 cents. Each dime is worth 10 cents, so 2 dimes equals 20 cents. Each penny is worth 1 cent, so 4 pennies equals 4 cents. A quarter is worth 25 cents. $10 + 20 + 4 + 25 = 59$ cents which can be rounded to 60 cents to match one of the provided answer selections.

15. C: Each number is 7 more than the previous number, so adding 7 to the previous number finds the next number. Thus, the fifth number is 256, the sixth number is 263, and the seventh number is 270.

16. B: The farmer plants 17 rows of corn each season. This can be found using all of the information given in the table. The farmer had planted 34 rows of corn by the end of Season 2 and 68 rows of corn by the end of Season 4, indicating an increase of 34 rows of corn between the two seasons. So, by dividing 34 by 2, the numbers of rows planted in one season is found. Also, the farmer had planted 102 rows of corn by the end of Season 6 and 136 rows of corn by the end of Season 8, indicating an increase of 17 rows of corn planted in one season. If 17 rows of corn are added to the number given at the end of Season 2, the result is 51 rows of corn planted by the end of Season 3. If another 17 rows of corn are added to this amount, the farmer would have planted 68 ears of corn by the end of Season 4, which he did. Thus, he did plant 17 rows of corn each year. He had planted 119 rows of corn by the end of Season 7, 153 rows of corn by the end of Season 9, and 170 rows of corn by the end of Season 10.

17. B: The place value is assigned by the position of the digit. The places from left to right are ones, tens, hundreds, thousands, ten-thousands, etc. The 4 is located in the tens place since it is two spaces from the left.

18. B: A number sentence that subtracts the number of friends from the total number of stamps will not provide the number of stamps needed to give each friend. Instead, an appropriate multiplication or division number sentence within the following fact family is needed: $9 \times 5 = 45$, $5 \times 9 = 45$, $45 \div 9 = 5$, or $45 \div 5 = 9$.

19. D: The pattern displayed is an arrow pointing right, left, up, right, left....so the next arrow should be pointing up to continue the pattern.

20. B: The number of blocks used in each tower increases by 2. Therefore, the number of blocks used in the next four towers can be found by adding 2 to the number of blocks in the 4th tower and continuing to add 2 blocks for each tower that comes next. This gives: 10, 12, 14, and 16, with 16 blocks used in the eighth tower.

21. D: The number of books brought by 2 students is 8, while the number of books brought by 5 students and 6 students increased by 4. Thus, the number of books brought by each student was 4. This fact can be checked by starting with 1 student and 4 books brought, and continuing the pattern to make sure it corresponds with the numbers in the table. For example, 8 students brought 32, which does in fact agree with the each student bringing 4 books. So, the number of books each student brought, 4, is multiplied by the number of students to find the total number of books that were brought. Thus, 12 students brought 12×4 books, or 48 books.

22. A: Each car has 4 wheels, so the numbers of cars should be multiplied by 4 to find the total number of wheels. 3 cars will have 3×4 wheels, or 12 wheels, 4 cars will have 4×4 wheels, or 16 wheels, 7 cars will have 7×4 wheels, or 28 wheels, 11 cars will have 11×4 wheels, or 44 wheels, and 12 cars will have 12×4 wheels, or 48 wheels.

23. A: The place value of a digit depends on its location in relation to the decimal point. The places to the left of the decimal are ones, tens, then hundreds, respectively. To round a number to a certain place value, look at the digit to the immediate right. If the digit to the right is 5 or more, round up by adding one followed by a zero. If the digit is less than five, round down by keeping the same digit followed by a zero. For this problem, the digit in the hundreds place is 2. The digit to its immediate right is 4. Since 4 is less than 5, round down. So, 49,249 rounded to the nearest hundred is 49,200.

24. A: One way to compare two fractions is by making two strip diagrams. The denominator represents how many equal spaces the strip will be divided into. The numerator represents how many spaces on the strip will be shaded in. It is important to make the strip diagrams the same size to accurately compare the fractions. When looking at the strip diagrams, it is evident that $\frac{1}{3}$ is less than $\frac{11}{12}$.

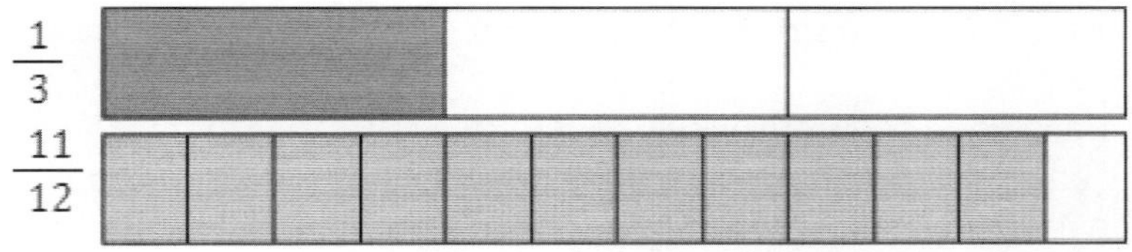

25. C: The number line shows three marks between each whole number, making 4 equal parts between each whole number. Point S is located at $14\frac{1}{2}$ since it is halfway between 14 and 15, or 2 marks to the right of 14, which can also be written as $14\frac{2}{4}$. $14\frac{3}{4}$ is greater than that number. It is easier to see which fraction is greater if the denominators are the same, since then, just the numerators are compared. So, $14\frac{3}{4}$ is $\frac{1}{4}$ more than the number shown on the number line, and this is the only choice that is greater than the value of Point S.

26. D: $\frac{6}{14}$ is the only value that comes between $\frac{3}{14}$ and $\frac{7}{14}$ on the number line. $\frac{1}{14}$ is less than $\frac{3}{14}$, so it is before $\frac{3}{14}$ on the number line. $\frac{3}{14}$ is equal to $\frac{3}{14}$, so it is at the exact place on the number line. $\frac{9}{14}$ is greater than $\frac{3}{14}$, so it is after $\frac{3}{14}$ on the number line.

27. C: The triangle shown for Choice C is congruent to the given triangle, since all side lengths and angles are congruent. Basically, the triangles must be the same size to be congruent, but can be flipped or rotated in any way.

28. A: A pentagon has 5 sides. An octagon has 8 sides. A nonagon has 9 sides. A decagon has 10 sides.

29. B: The place value of a digit depends on its location in relation to the decimal point. The places to the left of the decimal are ones, tens, then hundreds, respectively. To round a number to a certain place value, you look at the digit to the immediate right. If the digit to the right is 5 or more, round up by adding one. If the digit is less than five, round down by keeping the same digit. For this problem, the digit in the tens place is 0. The digit to its immediate right is 9. Since 9 is greater than 5, round up. So, 6,709 rounded to the nearest ten is 6,710.

30. C: A circle is a two-dimensional shape that is not a polygon. It does not have straight sides that meet at vertices. All of the other choices are two-dimensional polygons.

31. B: The perimeter is the sum of the lengths of all five sides, or $5 + 5 + 3 + 3 + 4$, which equals 20. Therefore, the perimeter of the pentagon is 20 cm.

32. C: $\frac{9}{12}$ is greater than $\frac{7}{12}$. They are not equal. When comparing fractions with the same denominator, compare only the values in the numerator. Since they share a common denominator of 12, compare only the 9 and 7. Since 9 is greater than 7, the same can be said for the fraction $\frac{9}{12}$ when compared to $\frac{7}{12}$.

33. C: The width of the notebook can be estimated by marking off lengths that are close to the measurement of a centimeter. The width of the book is slightly less than 5.5 cm, so it is about 5 cm.

34. D: The triangle includes 21 whole square units, plus 7 one-half square units, or $3\frac{1}{2}$ square units. So, 21 square units plus $3\frac{1}{2}$ square units gives a total of $24\frac{1}{2}$ square units.

35. B: One way to compare two fractions is by making two strip diagrams. The denominator represents how many equal spaces the strip will be divided into. The numerator represents how many spaces on the strip will be shaded in. It is important to make the strip diagrams the same size to accurately compare the fractions. When looking at the strip diagrams, it is evident that $\frac{2}{4}$ is equal to $\frac{5}{10}$.

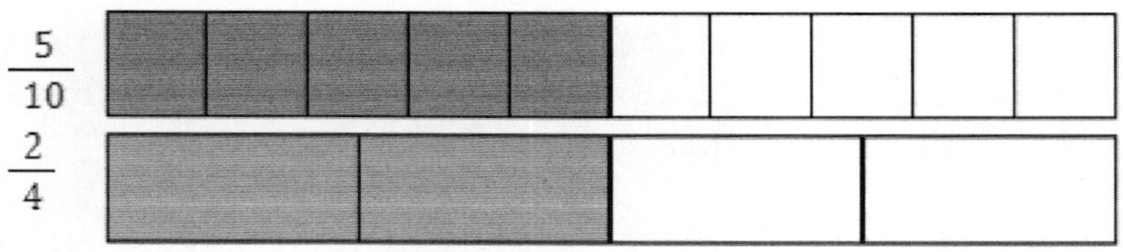

36. D: The thermometer shows 4 marks between each whole number, or 5 intervals. This means each interval on the thermometer represents 2 degrees since there are 5 intervals between each difference of 10 degrees. The thermometer reveals a reading at 4 degrees above 70 degrees (2

marks above 70), or 6 degrees below 80 degrees (3 marks below 80). Thus, the temperature outside is 74 degrees Fahrenheit.

37. A: The short hand, or hour hand, is between 10 o'clock and 11 o'clock, revealing that Amanda arrived after 10 o'clock, but before 11 o'clock. It is much closer to the 10, so this indicates the time is much closer to 10 o'clock than 11 o'clock. The long hand, or minute hand, is pointing to the 2, indicating 10 minutes after the hour. This is because for minutes, each number represents 5 minutes; so $2 \times 5 = 10$. So, she arrived at the party at 10:10.

38. B: Since there are sixty minutes in an hour, a "quarter" in time represents 15 minutes. A quarter past three would mean 15 minutes after 3 o'clock or 3:15. Represented on an analog clock, the big hand would be pointing to the three and the small hand pointing just past the three.

39. B: There are 6 yellow cards and 3 red cards. The more cards there are of a certain color, the more likely it is that the color is drawn. With more yellow cards than red cards in the bag, he is more likely to draw a yellow card than a red card. There are more green cards than yellow cards, so he is more likely to draw a green card than a yellow card. There are less yellow cards than blue cards, so he is less likely to draw a yellow card than a blue card. Finally, the number of red, blue, green, and yellow cards are all different – so none of them are equally likely to be drawn compared to another color. Thus, Choice B is the only true statement.

40. A: The pictograph for Choice A reveals that each picture of a cake represents 5 actual cakes. Therefore, the numbers given in the table, divided by 5, should equal the number of cakes represented in the pictograph. The pictograph accurately shows 5 cakes for 25 actual cakes, 3 cakes for 15 actual cakes, 7 cakes for 35 actual cakes, and 4 cakes for 20 actual cakes. This is the only pictograph that represents the correct number of cakes.

41. C: Florida had 20 teachers that attended the event, which is less than the number of teachers who attended the event from each of the other three states. The number of teachers that attended the event from each of the other states were 40 (Arizona), 80 (New York), and 50 (California). Also, just looking at the bar graph shows that Florida had the least number of teachers attend compared to the other states because the bar is much lower in the graph.

42. D: Since the spinner only has sections, labeled 1-8, there is not a section, labeled "9". Therefore, it is impossible for the spinner to land on a 9.

43. D: The correct order when order from greatest to least is 602; 592; 591; 588; 584; 573. 602 is the furthest to the right on the number line, so it is the largest. 573 is the furthest to the left on the number line, so it is the smallest.

44. 8: The hamster received 10 votes and the fish received 2 votes. The difference is $10 - 2 = 8$ votes.

Reading Practice Test#1

Questions 1 – 9 pertain to the following passage:

Miguel's World

Old Logs Help Animals

(1) Miguel Gonzalez and his father took many walks in the woods near their house. When Miguel was very young, around five, he liked to pick up branches and hit them against the ground and the trees. Sometimes he would waive the stick and pretend he was fighting a great battle. Mr. Gonzalez always told Miguel to drop the stick.

(2) "You will poke an eye out," said Mr. Gonzalez. A few years later, Miguel stopped hitting with sticks and started asking his father about the trees and other things he saw in the woods. Miguel's father told him how to identify different trees by the texture of their bark and the size and shape of their leaves. Miguel found out how trees spread their seeds and what kinds of animals eat the leaves, bark, and seeds. Miguel loved taking walks with his father, but he did not appreciate all the things that he saw in the woods. One day they almost tripped over a log that had fallen on the trail. Miguel kicked it.

(3) "Stupid log, it almost made me fall," he said. Miguel's father waved his arms, shook his head, and told his son to stop.

"That's not just a piece of wood, Miguel," said Mr. Gonzalez. "That log is a home for many creatures and plants. Kicking that log would be like an earthquake to them! How would you like it if a giant ant kicked our house?"

(4) "There are ants in there?" asked Miguel.

"Watch," said Mr. Gonzalez. He brushed the old brown leaves and rotting bark off the top of the log until they could see the wood buried underneath. On the smooth surface were clusters of small dark holes. An ant poked its head from one of the holes. Miguel laughed.

(5). "Is there anything else in that log?" Miguel asked.

"Let's see," said Mr. Gonzalez. The two brushed off more leaves. They worked carefully to avoid touching the slimy slugs that dotted the log. Near the end of the rotten piece of timber was a large rough hole. A squirrel darted out from the hole and chattered noisily. On the nearby trees, birds called and sang noisily, too.

(6) "They're waiting for us to leave so they can eat," smiled Mr. Gonzalez. "Those ants and slugs may not seem tasty to us, but they are a gourmet treat for the birds."

"Let's go," said Miguel. "They look hungry, and I hate making them wait for lunch."

(7) After a few minutes, Miguel turned suddenly and started walking quickly in the opposite direction, back toward the log.

"Hey, what are you doing? What's up?" called Miguel's father.

Miguel stopped and turned around. "We left the log uncovered. If we don't put the leaves and bark back where we found them, the ants won't have anywhere to hide."

(8) Miguel's father laughed and started to jog toward his son. "A little while ago you hated that log. Now you want to protect it."

"You always told me, treat others as you want to be treated," said Miguel with a smile. "I'm just following your advice!"

1. Paragraph 1 is mostly about:

a. The woods near Miguel's house
b. Miguel's father's love for nature
c. Miguel's behavior during walks
d. How sticks can be used as weapons

2. How did Miguel change when he got older?

a. He became more frightened of the woods
b. He became more dangerous toward his father
c. He became more bored with his father
d. He became more interested in the woods

3. Which meaning best fits the way the word identify is used in paragraph 2?

a. To become the same
b. To understand well
c. To recognize
d. To symbolize

4. Where does this story take place?

a. In a forest
b. In a park
c. In a garden
d. In an orchard

5. Which of the following words best describes Miguel's reaction when he learns that ants live in logs?

a. Happy
b. Confused
c. Angry
d. Sad

6. What is the title of this article?

a. Miguel Gonzalez
b. Miguel's World
c. Old Logs Help Animals
d. By Martha Gold

7. Read the chart below. It shows the order in which some events happened in the story.

Miguel played with sticks during walks in the woods with his father.
⇓
⇓
Miguel and his father walk away so the birds can eat the ants and slugs in the log.
⇓
Miguel runs back to the log to put the leaves and bark back on top of the log.

Which of the following statements belongs in the empty box?

a. Miguel's father tells him not to kick the log.
b. Miguel laughs at the ants.
c. Miguel gets angry and goes home.
d. Miguel's father sits on the log.

8. Which sentence from the story showed that Miguel changed his mind?

a. "You always told me, treat others as you want to be treated"
b. "A little while ago you hated that log. Now you want to protect it."
c. "They look hungry, and I hate making them wait for lunch."
d. "If we don't put the leaves and bark back where we found them, the ants won't have anywhere to hide."

9. What will Miguel probably do from now on if he comes across a log in the trail?

a. He will push the log out of the way
b. He will kick the log out of the way
c. He will turn back and walk home
d. He will look for animals in the log

Questions 10 – 15 pertain to the following passage:

My name is Tanya, and I have a dog whose name is Maize. I found her one summer in the parking lot of a supermarket when she was a puppy. I was taking our cart back to the store when I saw a small black and white animal dart under a row of shopping carts next to the main door. It moved so fast, all I saw was a blur. I did not know if the animal was a cat, a dog, or a skunk until it started barking.

My mom always told me not to play with strange animals, but something about Maize seemed safe. I bent down to find her under the carts and called to her. She came creeping out, slowly at first. Then she ran straight to me, wagging her tail. I picked her up and brought her back to my mom.

"Look what I found!" I said, holding up Maize, as she licked my face.

"No," said my mom.

I was about to protest when the puppy leaned over to my mom and licked her hand. Then she tried to lick my mom's face. My mom started to laugh.

"You are cute!" she said to the puppy. "It's hard to say no to a kiss like that."

"Can we keep her?" I asked.

"If you take care of her," said Mom. "You have to feed her, take her out for walks, and train her to behave."

At first, I was excited to have a dog. Maize slept on my bed and woke me up every morning by jumping on my bed. I took her for long walks in the park. Then school started, and I had to wake up early to take Maize outside before I got on the bus. I had to fill her food and water bowls as soon as I got home. I could not go to my friends' houses because I had to be home to take care of Maize. I started to wish I had not found Maize.

One Friday afternoon I was walking down my street when I saw my best friend, Laticia.

"Hey Tanya!" Laticia called. "Is that Maize?"

"Yes," I said.

"Wait here," said Laticia. "I am going to ask my mom if I can come over to play with you guys."

After a few minutes, Laticia came back. "Mom said I can come over for an hour, so let's go," she said.

We had a great time—Laticia, Maize, and me. Now my friends come over to my house to play all the time. They want to see me and play with Maize. I'm so glad I found Maize. She's the best friend a girl could have.

10. Which words help the reader understand the meaning of the word dart in the first paragraph?

a. Until it started barking
b. It moved so fast
c. A small black and white animal
d. Under a row

11. Why did Tanya think Maize was a skunk?

a. Skunks live under shopping carts.
b. Dogs are not black and white.
c. Skunks are black and white.
d. Tanya smelled something bad.

12. How did Tanya's walks with Maize change after school started?

a. Tanya had to walk to the park with Maize in the afternoon
b. Tanya woke up with Maize barking at her door
c. Tanya had to get up early to walk Maize before school
d. Tanya had to walk Maize after feeding her

13. What is the main problem in the story?

a. Tanya's mom won't let her keep Maize
b. Tanya's friends don't like Maize
c. Maize is messing up the house during the day
d. Tanya can't visit her friends after school

14. How did Laticia solve Tanya's problem?

a. Laticia went over to Tanya's house
b. Tanya went to Laticia's house
c. Tanya gave Maize away
d. Tanya and her mom went to the supermarket

15. What title would be the best choice for this story?

a. Tanya's New Best Friend
b. Maize is Crazy
c. Dogs are Difficult
d. Laticia Comes Over

Questions 16 – 20 pertain to the following passage:

The Animal Times

Bats: Our Flying Friends

Most people are afraid of bats. They are scared of their sharp teeth. They are scared because bats only come out at night. People worry that bats will bite them, but bats do not feed on people. Most bats in North America eat insects that they catch in the air with their teeth. Some bats eat mice, birds, frogs, lizards, and other bats. One kind of bat in Mexico catches fish in the claws of its hind legs. In Asia, large bats called Flying Foxes eat fruit. Other bats with long noses drink sweet juice from flowers.

All bats are mammals. They are the only mammals that fly. Bats live everywhere in the world except Antarctica and the North Pole. Most bats do not drink blood. Only vampire bats drink blood. Vampire bats live in Central and South America. They land on animals and bite them to make a tiny cut. Then they lap up the blood with their tongues. Vampire bats rarely bite people. If they do bite, they do not take much blood. However, bats may carry germs that cause disease.

Bats are not good pets, but they are useful to people. They eat insects, mice and other pests. Some cultures even think bats bring good luck!

16. Which of the following choices names the foods that bats eat?

a. fox, pets, cats, dogs
b. mice, blood, fish, insects
c. noses, teeth, claws, legs
d. flowers, seeds, nuts, grass

17. Why are people afraid of bats?

a. Bats have long noses
b. Bats catch fish in their claws
c. Bats only come out at night
d. Bats are not good pets

18. Where do bats NOT live?

a. Central and South America
b. Antarctica
c. Asia
d. North America

19. Look at the diagram below about flying foxes and vampire bats, and then answer the question that follows.

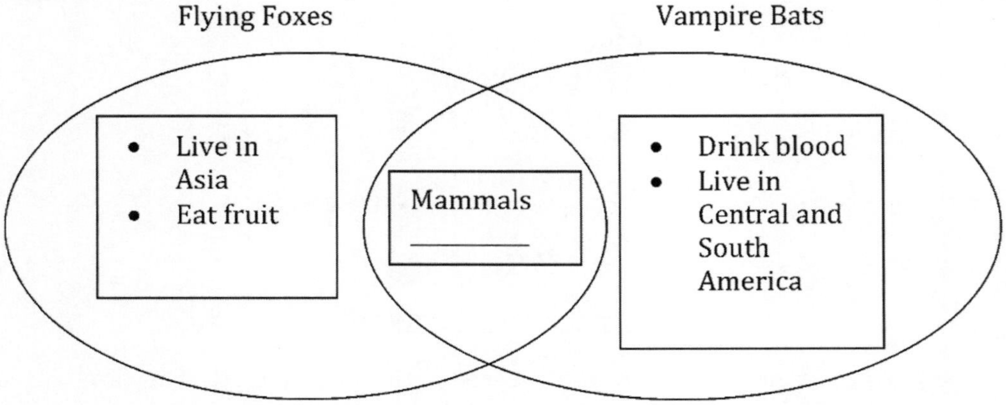

Which of the following belongs in the blank?

a. Bite animals and sometimes people
b. Eat insects
c. Make good pets
d. Only come out at night

20. What is the title of this article?

a. Bats: Our Flying Friends
b. Animal Times by Martha Gold
c. Animal Times
d. By Martha Gold

Questions 21 -27 pertain to the following passage:

Sam, My Teddy Bear

When I was just a child of three, I got a teddy bear.

With a squeeze, I called him Sam, and I took him everywhere,

to my grandma's, the babysitter's, the doctor's and the pool.

Sometimes big kids would laugh at me, but my friends thought Sam was cool.

But all that travel took its toll on Sam's good looks.

His fur wore off in patches and his ears bent into crooks.

Now he stays put on a shelf,

next to some blocks and a small green elf.

I still love Sam and would never give him away,

but I'm too old for teddy bears, so in my room he'll stay.

21. What choice best summarizes this poem?

a. Sam wore out after a few years. His fur was in patches and his ears were bent. He looked old
b. A girl got a teddy bear for a present and took it everywhere. Then she got bored with it
c. A girl got a teddy bear for a present and loved it. After taking it everywhere with her, she outgrew it, but she still loves it
d. The girl took the bear everywhere, to her grandmother's, the babysitter's and the pool. Kids laughed at her

22. How old was the author when she got the bear?

a. Three
b. Two
c. Four
d. Five

23. What did the author do when she first got the bear?

a. Laughed at him
b. Took him everywhere
c. Put him on a shelf
d. Gave him away

24. What choice shows how Sam looked after a few years?

a. "My friends thought Sam was cool"
b. "His fur wore off in patches"
c. "Sometimes big kids would laugh at me"
d. "Next to some blocks and a small, green elf"

25. What choice shows the author no longer takes Sam everywhere?

a. "All that travel had its toll on Sam's good looks"
b. "Next to some blocks and a small green elf"
c. "I still love Sam and would never give him away"
d. "But I'm too old for teddy bears, so in my room he'll stay"

26. In this poem, where are the rhyming words?

a. at the end of every other line
b. at the end of every very third line
c. at the end of every two lines
d. at the end of every three lines

27. What is the correct order of events in this poem?

a. Child receives Sam. Child takes Sam everywhere. Child puts Sam on a shelf
b. Child puts Sam on a shelf. Child takes Sam everywhere. Child receives Sam
c. Child takes Sam everywhere. Child receives Sam. Child puts Sam on a shelf
d. Child receives Sam. Child puts Sam on a shelf. Child takes Sam everywhere

Questions 28 – 34 pertain to the following passage:

Fire Needs Fuel and More to Burn

On the ground lay a dead tree, its branches sticking out like a porcupine's quills. Jake started breaking off the branches and putting them in a pile. His father had sent him to find kindling wood for their fire.

"What's kindling wood?" Jake asked.

"Boy! You've been living in the city too long, Jake!" said Jake's father. "Kindling is little branches no thicker around than this." He held up his hand and made a circle with his first finger and thumb. "We need them to start the fire."

Jake measured the circumference of the branches by wrapping his first finger and thumb around each one. If the thumb and finger touched, he put it in the pile. If his finger and thumb could not touch, he left it on the tree. After he had collected an armful, Jake brought the pile of branches to his father.

His father was crumpling newspaper and arranging it around the cement circle that held up an iron grill. The wood was dry, brown, and old, but not rotten.

"Perfect kindling, Jake," said his father. "Good job!"

He piled the kindling on top of the newspapers and lit a match. The flames crept up the corners and edges of the paper and curled around the sticks. Soon the flames were flickering, and Jake's father put on the first log.

"What makes fire burn?" asked Jake, as he set out plates and cups on the picnic table for dinner.

"Three things," said his father. "I'll give you a hint. You are breathing one of them right now."

"Smoke?" asked Jake, coughing.

"Oxygen," said Jake's father, laughing. "The wood we're using is another. Wood is fuel, paper is fuel, and gasoline is fuel. Anything that can burn is fuel. Finally, you need high heat, called the kindling temperature, so the fuel will catch fire and make flames."

"How hot does the kindling temperature have to be?" asked Jake.

"It's different for different kinds of fuel," said Jake's father. "For wood it is about 500°F (260°C). Some fuels need a higher kindling temperature, and some need a lower temperature."

Jake looked down at the fire. The flames crept around the log and started to catch on to the bark. The flames flickered around the iron bars, but the bars did not burn.

"Why doesn't the iron in the grill burn?" asked Jake.

"It's fireproof," said Jake's father. "Oxygen cannot mix with it, so it cannot burn. It is the same with stone or brick."

"It's a good thing," said Jake, as he unwrapped the hotdogs. "Or we would have to order out for pizza!"

28. Where are Jake and his father?

a. In a cabin
b. At a campsite
c. At a lake
d. Next to a river

29. In the second paragraph, what does the word circumference mean?

a. The distance around a circle
b. The distance across a circle
c. The distance across a stick
d. The distance along a stick

30. What was good about the kindling that Jake collected?

a. It was wet, young, and green
b. It was dry, rotten, and brown
c. It was dry, old, and brown
d. It was wet, old, and brown

31. What is the right combination to make fire?

a. Fuel + food + air
b. Fuel + kindling heat + wood
c. Fuel + oxygen + food
d. Fuel + oxygen + kindling heat

32. What is the order of events in this story?

a. Jake takes out hotdogs. Jake gets kindling wood. Jake's father starts the fire
b. Jake's father starts the fire. Jake takes out hotdogs. Jake gets kindling wood
c. Jake's father starts the fire. Jake gets kindling wood. Jake takes out hotdogs
d. Jake gets kindling wood. Jake's father starts the fire. Jake takes out hotdogs

33. How hot is the kindling temperature for wood?

a. 600°F
b. 260°F
c. 500°F
d. 700°F

34. What does the small round circle after the temperature mean?

a. Hot
b. Temperature
c. Degrees
d. Cold

Refer to the passage "Linda Richards: Medical Pioneer" to answer questions 35-40.

Linda Richards: Medical Pioneer

(1) There are people whose job is to take care of us while we're being treated by doctors. These people are called nurses, and they have helped hundreds of millions of Americans feel better and get well faster over the years. All of us should be grateful for nurses because nearly all of us have been helped by a nurse at one time or another, and we all have several family members who have been brought back to health thanks to the efforts of nurses. Linda Richards is one of the pioneers of modern nursing.

(2) Linda Richards was born in West Potsdam, New York, in 1841. Her father was a preacher, and he wanted Linda to become a missionary when she grew up. However, her father died when she was only four years old. Then, her mother became very sick, and Linda spent years taking care of her mother. Linda's mother died when Linda was fourteen. Linda had enjoyed taking care of her mother, and Linda decided that she was going to become a nurse, not a missionary.

(3) Linda Richards was not the first nurse in the world by any stretch of the imagination. Nurses have been around for centuries, but, until recently, nursing was a lot different than it is today. Back in the old days, most nurses were not well educated. Some of them couldn't read or write, and they knew little about medicine or health. They mostly did things to make patients feel more comfortable, such as give them a drink of water, help them go to the bathroom, or wipe their foreheads with a wet rag. These tasks are very important, but there is a lot more a nurse needs to know and do to help people get well. Linda Richards understood that, and she helped change nursing into the modern profession it is today.

(4) After helping a local doctor for a while, she took a nursing job at a hospital in Boston, but it was an awful experience. There was no training, and nurses were expected to work from 6 in the morning to 9:30 at night. They also had to sleep at the hospital, near their patients. They would have to get up every time a patient

called them. This was very hard on nurses, and many of them quit, including Linda. She soon became a student in the first class ever held at America's very first nursing school. After she graduated, she became a supervisor at Bellevue Hospital in New York City. While she worked there, she invented a way of keeping records for each patient. At the time, most hospitals did not keep very good track of their patients and their health. However, Linda Richards changed all of that. Before long, all hospitals in America were keeping patient records.

(5) Linda Richards didn't stop there. She kept getting more education for herself. She even went to England to study with Florence Nightingale, one of the most famous nurses in history. After she returned to America, she began starting nursing schools across the country. At these schools, she trained people in the modern methods of nursing. Pretty soon, nurses who had an education in medicine were helping patients all over America. Linda Richards's efforts greatly improved nursing in America. Thanks to her, millions of people have lived longer and better lives.

35. Which of these words has a similar meaning to *pioneer*?

a. Follower
b. Inventor
c. Traveler
d. Patient

36. Which of the definitions above matches the way that *record* is used in paragraph 4?

Record (*noun)*
pronounced: reh-kord

1. a vinyl disc that can be used to play music
2. an album of songs by a band or musician
3. the best performance of a task or feat
4. a written or typed copy of information

a. Definition 1
b. Definition 2
c. Definition 3
d. Definition 4

37. What is the main idea of paragraph 3?

a. Linda Richards was not actually the first person to become a nurse.
b. Linda Richards became a nurse instead of becoming a missionary.
c. Linda Richards worked to make needed improvements to nursing.
d. Linda Richards wanted to teach nurses to read and write.

38. What is the passage's main idea?

a. Linda Richards decided to become a nurse after caring for her mother.
b. Linda Richards invented a way for hospitals to keep better records.
c. Linda Richards was one of the first educated nurses in America.
d. Linda Richards worked hard to solve problems she saw in the field of nursing.

39. Why is paragraph 2 organized using a chronological pattern?

a. It describes the events that led Linda Richards to become a nurse.
b. It tells of the problem that Linda Richards wanted to solve as a nurse.
c. It explains the effects of Linda Richards becoming a nurse.
d. It shows why the reader should become a nurse.

40. Which sentence from the passage shows that Linda Richards helped others become better nurses?

a. Linda decided that she was going to become a nurse, not a missionary.
b. While she worked there, she invented a way of keeping records for each patient.
c. At these schools, she trained people in the modern methods of nursing.
d. Thanks to her, millions of people have lived longer and better lives.

Answer Key and Explanations for Reading Test #1

1. C: The first paragraph mostly describes Miguel's behavior and actions as a five-year-old during walks with his father. "...he liked to pick up branches and hit them against the ground and the trees. Sometimes he would waive the stick and pretend he was fighting a great battle."

2. D: Miguel showed more interest in the woods by asking his father questions about different trees and plants. As a result of his interest, Miguel learned how to identify trees by their bark and leaves and how trees reproduce by spreading their seeds to other parts of the forest.

3. C: In this paragraph, the word identify is used to show the action of recognizing, or identifying by sight, different trees and plants by the appearance of their bark or leaves. It is different from understanding well because Miguel doesn't have to understand trees very well to identify their leaves and bark.

4. A: This story takes place in a forest. Several hints in the story indicate its location, including mention of taking walks in the woods. Woods is another word for forest. Also, orchards tend to have the same kinds of trees, and gardens and parks tend to be tended neatly without rotting logs lying around.

5. B: Miguel is confused because he did not think of the rotten log as being useful for anyone or anything. He kicked the log for this reason. The news that it served as a home for different insects did not match his impression that rotten logs just take up space and make walking on trails difficult. He was angry when he almost tripped over the log, but he did not stay angry for long. He was neither happy nor sad.

6. C: The title is located in straight black letters below the name of the publication, Miguel's World. The words "By Martha Gold" in the heading tell who wrote the article.

7. A: In the story, Miguel's father tells him not to kick the log after we learned that he used to play with sticks when he was younger and before Miguel and his father leave the log and Miguel returns to replace the bark and leaves they brushed aside.

8. B: Miguel's father points out how Miguel's attitude toward the log changes. Usually, people love things that they want to protect. Hating something is usually the opposite of wanting to protect it.

9. D: Miguel already was interested in the plants and animals in the woods. Now that he has learned what lives inside old logs, he probably will look for them the next time he comes across an old log lying on the ground.

10. B: The sentence after the one with the word dart starts with the phrase "it moved so fast." The phrase "it moved so fast" relates to the previous verb, dart.

11. C: The animal moved so quickly that at first, Tanya only could see the animals' colors and not its shape. Maize was a puppy at the time and about the size of a fully-grown skunk, which happens to be black and white.

12. C: The story says that after school started, Tanya was no longer able to take Maize out for walks during the day. Instead, she had to get up early so she could take Maize out for a walk before going to school.

13. D: Tanya promised her mother that she would take care of Maize. As part of that promise, Tanya had to be home every day to help feed and take care of her dog. Tanya could not go over to her friends' houses after school. After a while Tanya began to miss seeing her friends outside of school.

14. A: Laticia helped solve Tanya's problem by inviting herself over to Tanya's house. This way, Tanya could see her friends and take care of her dog at the same time.

15. A: This title best summarizes the story's main idea that Maize started to look like a burden, but turned out to be a great friend by helping Tanya keep up with her friends after school. The other titles either are inaccurate (Maize is not crazy) or focused too narrowly on one aspect of the story.

16. B: The story lists the things different kinds of bats eat, including mice, blood, fish and insects.

17. C: People are afraid of bats for many reasons. One reason is that bats only come out at night when it is dark, and people tend to be nervous about animals that they cannot see.

18. B: Bats live everywhere where there are plants. For that reason, the only places you will not find bats are Antarctica and the North Pole, since those areas are too cold for plants.

19. D: The space in the middle of a Venn diagram lists the components that the two sides of the diagram have in common. Both kinds of bats only come out at night.

20. A: The title is the straight, solid name under the name of the publication. It is specific to the article, whereas "Animal Times" is more general and refers to the title of the publication, not the article.

21. C: This choice best summarizes the main idea of the poem, which is about a child at first adoring a toy, but eventually outgrowing it. Like lots of children, she stopped playing with the toy, but kept it for the memories and out of affection for the toy.

22. A: In the first line the author says she was three when she first got the bear.

23. B: The author took the bear everywhere with her when she first got it as a present.

24. B: "His fur wore off in patches" shows how the girl's constant handling wore the bear out.

25. D: "But now I'm too old for teddy bears, so in my room he'll stay" shows that while the author still loves the bear, she now keeps him in her room instead of taking him with her.

26. C: In this poem, the rhyming words are at the end of every two lines.

27. A: The correct order of events in this poem is: Child receives Sam. Child takes Sam everywhere. Child puts Sam on a shelf.

28. B: While one can eat food cooked by a fire in any of those places, the presence of a picnic table, old trees (where Jake collected kindling) and the grill indicate that they were at a campsite. Additionally, the passage made no mention of water, so it was not by a river or lake.

29. A: By wrapping his finger and thumb in a circle shape around the branches, Jake illustrated the concept of circumference, which is the measure around a circle.

30. C: The kindling that Jake collected was pronounced good by his father because it was old, dry, and brown. Rotten wood burns too quickly. Green wood or wet wood does not burn. Instead, it only smokes.

31. D: A fire needs fuel, oxygen, and kindling heat to burn. Food is another name for fuel, and fire specifically needs oxygen.

32. D: In the story Jake gets wood first, then his father starts the fire, and finally Jake gets out hot dogs to cook on the fire.

33. C: The story states specifically that the kindling temperature for wood is 500°F.

34. C: The small circle symbol after the number ° is read as "degrees." The number, the symbol, and the letter after it together are the temperature. Hot and cold are indicated by specific temperatures, not by symbols in the temperature.

35. B: The passage title calls Linda Richards a *pioneer*. The central idea of the passage is how Linda Richards tried new things that improved nursing. It even tells how she invented a new way for hospitals to keep records. This shows that Linda Richards was an *inventor*. This is a synonym of *pioneer*, so choice B is correct. Linda Richards did not simply follow what others did. She chose her own career and looked for new and better ways to help patients. She was not a follower, so choice A is incorrect. Linda Richards lived in a few places and traveled to England to learn from Florence Nightingale. However, the central idea of the passage is not that she was a traveler, so choice C is incorrect. The passage says that Linda Richards cared for patients but does not say that she was a patient. This means choice D is incorrect.

36. D: Paragraph 4 says that, before Linda Richards's invention, hospitals did not keep good track of patients and their health. Patient records were used to solve this problem. This means that records must help people keep track of information. One way to do this is to write down or type information so it can be read later. This matches Definition 4, so choice D is the correct answer. Paragraph 4 does not mention music or being entertained, so choices A and B are incorrect. The hospital did not need to compare how well different patients performed tasks or feats, so choice C is incorrect.

37. C: Paragraph 3 explains that, before Linda Richards's lifetime, nurses could not do much to help their patients. The paragraph ends by saying that Linda Richards helped fix this problem. Linda Richards helped make needed changes that improved nursing, so choice C is correct. Choice A says Linda Richards was not the first nurse. This is just a detail from the paragraph. It is not what the paragraph is about, so choice A is incorrect. Linda Richards's decision to become a nurse instead of a missionary is only mentioned in paragraph 2. This makes Choice B incorrect. The passage does not say that Linda Richards tried to teach anyone to read or write, meaning Choice D is incorrect.

38. D: The passage explains how Linda Richards became a nurse, saw that there were problems in nursing, and worked to learn more so she could help improve nursing. This means that choice D is correct. Caring for her mother was what inspired Linda Richards to become a nurse. During her early career, she invented a better record-keeping method. She was also one of the first nurses in America to go to nursing school. While all of these are facts mentioned in the passage, they are supporting details. Each of these facts is only mentioned once or twice. None of these ideas are the central idea of the passage, so choices A, B, and C are incorrect.

39. A: Paragraph 2 tells the reader some events that happened during Linda Richards's childhood. One of these events is the death of her father. Linda Richards's father wanted her to become a missionary. However, he was no longer alive to tell her to become a missionary instead of a nurse. Another event was her mother becoming sick. Linda Richards took care of her mother, and this experience made her want to become a nurse. These events caused Linda Richards to become a nurse, so choice A is correct. Linda Richards did not know about the problems in nursing until after these events, so choice B is incorrect. The effects of Linda Richards's career as a nurse also occurred after these events, so choice C is incorrect. This paragraph simply describes events that happened. It does not tell the reader reasons why it is good to become a nurse, so choice D is incorrect.

40. C: The sentence in choice C shows that Linda Richards taught others new methods for nursing. By doing this, she helped others become better nurses, so choice C is correct. The event in choice A occurred before Linda Richards began teaching other nurses, so choice A is incorrect. The sentence in choice B describes Linda Richards's invention. This invention helped doctors, nurses, and patients. However, it did not show others how to become better nurses, so choice B is incorrect. The sentence in choice D shows that Linda Richards's actions have helped millions of patients. Since this sentence shows that she helped patients instead of how she helped nurses, choice D is incorrect.

Reading Practice Test #2

Questions 1–9 refer to the following passage:

Snacks Made Easy

After school, Mika came running from the school bus into her house.

Mom, I'm starving," she said, dropping her school bag on the kitchen floor and opening the refrigerator. "What do we have to eat?"

"Not much," said her mother. "I have to go shopping today."

"Do we still have those cheese crackers?" asked Mika.

"We're all out," said Mika's mother. "If you want, we can make some."

"MAKE them?" asked Mika. "You mean with cheese and stuff?"

"There is a recipe I want to try," said Mika's mother. "Why don't we make some? Then we can go shopping."

"But I want something NOW," whined Mika.

"Have some fruit," said her mother, holding out an apple.

"Okay," said Mika, taking the apple. "Now, how do you make these crackers?"

Mika's mother put a sheet of paper on the kitchen table in front of her. On the paper was a recipe, or directions, on how to make cheese crackers.

<u>Cheese Crackers</u>

<u>Ingredients:</u>

- 1-cup all-purpose flour and a little
- Extra flour to roll out dough
- 1/2-teaspoon salt
- 4 tablespoons cold butter
- 8 ounces grated cheese
- (Cheddar or Monterey Jack)
- 1/4-cup of water

COOKING UTENSILS:

- 1 large mixing bowl
- 1 measuring cup
- 1/2-teaspoon measure
- Mixing spoon
- Rolling pin
- Cookie cutters
- 2 table knives or potato masher

DIRECTIONS:

- Heat the oven to 350° F.
- Cut the butter into small pieces.
- Mix the flour and salt together in a large bowl.
- Add the butter and cut it into the flour using two table knives or a potato masher. Cut until the pieces of butter are smaller than a pea.
- Add the water gradually, one tablespoon at a time. Mix it in until the dough sticks together in a ball.
- Cover the bowl with plastic wrap. Put it in the refrigerator for half-an-hour.
- Sprinkle flour on a clean table or on the counter. Put the dough in the middle of the flour.
- Roll out the dough until it is as thick as a regular-sized magazine. Cut out shapes using small cookie cutters.
- Place the shapes on a greased, non-stick cookie sheet. Bake for 15 minutes, or until the crackers are golden brown. Let cool and enjoy!

1. What is the title of this story?

a. Snacks Made Easy
b. Cheese Crackers
c. By Martha Gold
d. Snacks Made Easy By Martha Gold

2. Why did Mika's mother want to make cheese crackers?

a. Because Mika was hungry
b. Because they were out of cheese crackers
c. Because Mika's mother wanted to try a new recipe
d. Because Mika didn't want an apple

3. What did Mika mean when she said, "But I want something NOW," after her mother asked to make crackers?

a. Mika did not want cheese crackers
b. Mika wanted an apple
c. Mika wanted to go shopping
d. Mika was hungry

4. What does the word "ingredient" mean?

a. A statement that tells how to do something
b. One of the items used to make a food.
c. The temperature at which the food should bake
d. A name for the recipe

5. What ingredient would you need in order to complete step 2?

a. Flour
b. Butter
c. Salt
d. Pepper

6. Which of the following meanings best fits the way gradually is used in step 5?

a. A little at a time
b. Slowly
c. Not steep
d. Continuously

7. Why did the author number the steps in the directions?

a. Because letters were too confusing
b. To know how long the recipe takes to make
c. To show that it is important to complete the steps in order
d. For cooks who prefer to read numbers

8. Which answer should go in the blank?

What happens	Why it happens
Mika reads the cheese crackers recipe.	____________

a. Mika wants to make cheese crackers
b. Mika wants to go shopping
c. Mika wants another apple
d. Mika wants a different snack

9. What will Mika probably do in the future when she wants cheese crackers?

a. Open the refrigerator and look for them
b. Ask her mother to buy some at the store
c. Ask her mother to help her make some
d. Eat an apple instead

Questions 10–18 refer to the following passage:

An Unforgettable Day at the History Museum

Hakeem's third-grade class takes a field trip every spring to the county historical museum. The county historian gives the class a tour and afterward sets the students loose to explore the museum. Hakeem's older brother, Gerard, went two years earlier. Gerard said the museum was great except for one room.

"Watch out for the room with the old war uniforms, it's haunted," said Gerard at dinner one night.

"What do you mean, haunted?" asked Hakeem.

"We heard funny noises in the room," said Gerard. "We looked around to see if anyone else was there, but it was empty. Then Sammy swore he saw the eyes of one of the costume dummies move around, as if it were watching us. We were so scared we left before we got to the end of the exhibit."

"Gerard, stop scaring your brother," said Hakeem's mother. "Hakeem, there is no such thing as ghosts. I'm sure there is a logical explanation for those noises. As for the eyes moving, that's just Sammy's imagination getting out of hand."

Stories about ghosts usually do not frighten Hakeem. He laughed at all the ghost stories his counselor told at camp last summer around the campfire. He watched scary movies with his babysitter and felt fine. But something about Gerard's words made Hakeem feel uneasy. Gerard does not usually joke around. Hakeem doubted that Gerard was just trying to scare him. Instead, Gerard was probably trying to warn him.

On the day of the field trip, Hakeem asked his teacher, Mr. Orwell, about Gerard's story as they rode the bus to the museum.

"It's an old building," said Mr. Orwell. "The floor boards creak and I'm sure there are other parts of the museum that make strange noises. It's not haunted, just a little creepy."

"What about the eyes watching Sammy?" asked Hakeem.

Mr. Orwell laughed. "Sammy's got a great imagination," he said. "I'm sure that's what made him think the statue was watching him."

After the tour, Hakeem walked around the museum with his best friend Malcolm. Malcolm wanted to see the old war uniforms, but Hakeem was nervous. Finally, he agreed to follow his friend into the room. There were just a few standing lamps and one small bulb on the ceiling to provide light. Ten life-size dummies, or mannequins, each one wearing a different war uniform, stood in the dim room. As Hakeem walked by a mannequin, the overhead light flickered. At that moment, Hakeem looked at the mannequin's face. The flickering light made the shadows over its eyes jump. Hakeem gasped.

"What is it?" asked Malcolm.

"Watch," said Hakeem. They stood in front of the mannequin and waited. After a minute, the light overhead flickered.

"Whoa!" said Malcolm. "That looked like he was shifting his eyes!"

"That explains what Sammy saw," said Hakeem. "What about the noises?"

Malcolm started leaning from side to side and walked around the room like a duck. Each time he shifted his weight to one side, a floorboard creaked. As he wobbled around the room, the floorboards creaked and moaned.

Hakeem laughed. "This place is great!" he said. "I'm so glad my brother didn't scare me away!

10. Where does Hakeem's third-grade class go on a field trip every spring?

a. To a park
b. To an art museum
c. To a science museum
d. To a historical museum

11. What did Hakeem's brother Gerard warn him about?

a. The old war uniforms room
b. The old records room
c. The old costume dummies room
d. The old museum room

12. Which statement in paragraph 2 shows that Hakeem's mother does not trust Sammy?

a. Gerard, stop scaring your brother
b. Hakeem, there is no such thing as ghosts
c. I'm sure there is a logical explanation to those noises
d. That's just Sammy's imagination getting out of hand

13. What word best matches the description of Hakeem in paragraph three?

a Honest
b. Happy
c. Brave
d. Angry

14. What word best matches the description of Gerard in paragraph three?

a. Happy
b. Honest
c. Angry
d. Brave

15. What made the mannequin's eyes look like they were moving?

a. The few standing lamps
b. The creaky floorboards
c. The flickering overhead bulb
d. The old uniform

16. What definition best matches the meaning of the word dim in paragraph five?

a. Badly lit
b. Dusty
c. Empty
d. Crowded

17. Why did Hakeem laugh in paragraph seven?

a. Because Malcolm walked like a duck in the old uniform room
b. Because the old uniform room was haunted
c. Because his brother, Gerard, lied to him about the old uniform room
d. Because he found out the old uniform room was not haunted

18. Which of the following statements tells the main idea of this story?

a. It is important to be brave
b. Appearances can be deceiving
c. Trust people older than you
d. Historical museums are haunted

Questions 19–25 refer to the following passage:

One Giant Leap for Mankind

(1) On July 20, 1969, Neil Armstrong became the first man to walk on the moon, as 500 million people around the world watched on television. This was truly a historic event. Almost all people throughout history would have laughed at the idea that, one day, a man would walk on the moon. They would have said it was impossible. They would have called a person "crazy" for even talking about the idea. But, on July 20, 1969, a man from a small Ohio town proved them wrong.

Armstrong's Childhood

(2) Neil Armstrong was born on August 5, 1930, in Wapakoneta, Ohio. His father had to travel for his job, so the Armstrong family moved about 20 times while Neil was a boy. They moved back to Wapakoneta permanently when he was 14. By this time, Neil was in love with flying. Airplanes were still new back then, and most people had never been in one, but Neil took his first plane ride when he was only six years old. He fell in love with flying, and when he was a teenager, he started taking flying lessons. He even got a license to fly before he was old enough to get a driver's license! He was also active in Boy Scouts and earned its highest rank of Eagle Scout.

Armstrong's Early Career

(3) Neil went off to college at Purdue University in Indiana right after he turned 17. He studied for two years and then served in the Navy, where he became a fighter pilot. After fighting in the Korean War, he came back to finish his college degree. After college, he joined the Air Force and became a pilot who tested new kinds of aircraft. During his career, he flew in over 200 different kinds of vehicles. It was during this time that the government created NASA to explore space, and, in 1962, Neil Armstrong was selected to train as an astronaut.

First Man on the Moon

(4) In 1961, President John F. Kennedy announced that he wanted NASA to land on the moon before 1970. That meant Neil Armstrong and the other astronauts had to work hard to get ready. The work was very dangerous, and some men died while exploring space. Neil Armstrong and the other astronauts bravely continued, though, and Neil was selected to be the first human being to set foot on the moon. After they returned to Earth, he and the other astronauts became national heroes.

ARMSTRONG'S LATER LIFE

(5) Neil Armstrong could have used his fame to make a lot of money or run for president. Instead, he chose to live a quiet life out of the spotlight and became a college professor. He didn't go on TV or give interviews very often, and he didn't like traveling around giving speeches. He died on August 25, 2012, at age 82. Many people lead remarkable lives, but Neil Armstrong's life was truly "out of this world."

19. Which phrase below means the same thing as *permanently* in paragraph 2?

a. On time
b. Before dark
c. For good
d. At the same time

20. Notice that the passage has four sections, titled "Armstrong's Childhood," "Armstrong's Early Career," "First Man on the Moon," and "Armstrong's Later Life." Which of the following pieces of information would be found in the "First Man on the Moon" section?

a. Where Neil Armstrong attended high school
b. How old Neil Armstrong was when he got married
c. What year Neil Armstrong walked on the moon
d. How many siblings Neil Armstrong had

21. How is this passage organized?

a. It describes the history of NASA up until Neil Armstrong walked on the moon.
b. It tells how Neil Armstrong's favorite teacher inspired him to become an astronaut.
c. It explains how Neil Armstrong figured out how to fly a spaceship to the moon.
d. It shows how the events in Neil Armstrong's life led to him being the first man to walk on the moon.

22. What do the section titles "Armstrong's Childhood," "Armstrong's Early Career," "First Man on the Moon," and "Armstrong's Later Life" tell the reader?

a. Where Neil Armstrong lived during the events described in each section
b. Which part of Neil Armstrong's life each section is about
c. Where Neil Armstrong worked during the events described in each section
d. Which of Neil Armstrong's missions each section is about

23. Which of these definitions matches the way degree is used in paragraph 3?

Degree (*noun*) pronounced: dih-gree 1. the unit for a measurement of heat 2. how much of a certain quality something has 3. a confirmation that someone has graduated from college 4. the measurement of an angle

a. Definition 1
b. Definition 2
c. Definition 3
d. Definition 4

24. What is the main idea of paragraph 5?

a. Neil Armstrong chose to live a humble life after his time as an astronaut.
b. Neil Armstrong was shy person, so he avoided interviews and public appearances.
c. Neil Armstrong did not know enough about politics to run for president.
d. Neil Armstrong was not a successful astronaut, so he was not very famous.

25. Which of the following conclusions is supported by this passage?

a. All astronauts have a college degree and a pilot's license.
b. Neil Armstrong will be remembered as a historical figure.
c. All astronauts since Neil Armstrong have walked on the moon.
d. Neil Armstrong and President Kennedy became good friends.

Questions 26–29 refer to the following passage:

When I Am Sick

At least once a year my nose gets red,
and I cough and sniffle and sneeze.
My mother tucks me into bed
with a heavy blanket, so I won't freeze.
She feeds me a teaspoon of medicine,
it is purple and very thick.
It tastes like grapes and drips on my chin,
but it makes me feel better quick.
My mother stays home from work,
she reads me books and lets me watch TV.
I do not like feeling sick,
but I love having my mother all to me.

26. What kind of illness is the author describing in the first two lines?

a. Stomach flu
b. Headache
c. Mumps
d. Cold

27. What does the mother do when the author is sick?

a. Takes her temperature
b. Tucks her into bed
c. Calls the doctor
d. Makes tea

28. What does the medicine look and taste like?

a. Purple, thin, grapes and apples
b. Purple, thick, grapes and apples
c. Purple, thick, and grapes
d. Purple, thin, and grapes

29. What does the author like about being sick?

a. She gets her mother's full attention
b. She gets to stay home from school
c. She gets to watch TV
d. Her mother reads her books

Questions 30–34 refer to the following passage:

Our Neighbor Mercury

(1) Earth is a planet with many neighbors. Besides Earth, there are seven other full-sized planets in the solar system, and the one that is the closest to the Sun is named Mercury. Earth is about two and a half times the size of Mercury. The surface of Mercury is very rough, like our moon. There are lots of craters, and it is completely barren, with nothing but soil as far as the eye can see. Do you know how Mercury got its name? The name comes from Ancient Rome, some 24 centuries ago. The Romans believed in many different gods, and the messenger of the gods was called Mercury. He was able to move extremely fast. Because this planet moves around the Sun faster than the other planets, it was given the name Mercury.

(2) Sometimes, Mercury is closer to our planet than at other times, but it is always a long way away. The closest it ever gets to us is about 40 million miles. It is much closer to the Sun than Earth is, so it doesn't take nearly as long to revolve around the Sun. In fact, it only takes 88 days for Mercury to orbit the Sun. Here on Earth, a year is 365 days long, but, on Mercury, a year is only 88 days long. This means that if you're 10 years old on Earth, you would be almost 42 years old if you lived on Mercury!

(3) If that's not strange enough, consider this: Earth orbits around the Sun, and it also rotates, like a spinning top. One full rotation is 24 hours, or one day. Mercury also rotates, but much more slowly. A day on Mercury is 58 Earth days. Since a year on Mercury is only 88 Earth days, that means there are only one and a half "days" in a Mercury year. That would be like the Sun coming up on Earth and then it being

sunny 24 hours a day for four months, and then dark for four months straight, and then sunny again for four months. That would be very hard to get used to. Living on Mercury, where a day is 58 Earth days long, would be quite a change.

(4) Of course, there's no chance that anyone will ever actually live on Mercury. It's impossible due to the temperatures on the planet. Temperatures can range from 300 degrees below zero to around 800 degrees. 800 degrees is hot enough to melt some metals. We would broil to death almost instantly on Mercury. When it got dark, we would freeze to death. Some people believe that, one of these days, an astronaut will walk on Mars, but that will never happen on Mercury!

30. What is the main purpose of this passage?

a. To explain how long a year is
b. To discuss the entire solar system
c. To give facts about the Sun
d. To give facts about the planet Mercury

31. What word below means the same thing as barren **in paragraph 1?**

a. Blue
b. Round
c. Lifeless
d. Gigantic

32. In paragraph 1, what does *Ancient* mean?

a. Far away
b. Very old
c. Recent
d. Fictional

33. Which of the following statements describes the main idea of paragraph 4?

a. One day on Mercury is almost as long as one day on Earth.
b. Humans cannot survive on Mercury due to the temperatures.
c. Mercury is extremely hot because it is so close to the Sun.
d. Mercury only has two seasons: summer and winter.

34. Which of the following is true about the diagram of the solar system?

a. The author included the diagram to show how Mercury was discovered.
b. The author included the diagram to show why Mercury is named *Mercury*.
c. The author included the diagram to show how close Mercury is to the Sun.
d. The author included the diagram to show what life would be like on Mercury.

Question 35 does not have an associated passage:

35. Which TWO of the following words are synonyms with "inquisitive."

Peter always enjoyed going to the zoo. He was so <u>inquisitive</u> about animals that he had never seen before.

a. Curious
b. Imaginative
c. Honest
d. Interested
e. Afraid

Questions 36–40 refer to the following passage:

Patricio Suarez

Come To My Birthday Party

When: Saturday, February 12, 2011 at 2 p.m.
Where: 1234 Main Street, El Paso

Bring: Your bathing suit

Reply: (915) 123-4567

Email: Suarez@abcde.com

36. Who is having a party?

a. Saturday February
b. Main Street
c. Your bathing suit
d. Patricio Suarez

37. Where is the location for the party?

a. (915) 123-4567
b. 1234 Main Street, El Paso
c. Suarez@abcde.com
d. Your bathing suit

38. What time is the party?

a. 2 p.m.
b. 11 a.m.
c. 3 p.m.
d. 1 p.m.

39. What kind of party is it?

a. Welcome home
b. Anniversary
c. Graduation
d. Birthday

40. What is the main activity at the party?

a. Playing games
b. Eating cake
c. Swimming
d. Horseback riding

Answer Key and Explanations for Reading Test #2

1. A: "Snacks Made Easy" is the title of the story. "Cheese Crackers" is the name of the recipe, and "By Martha Gold" tells who wrote the story.

2. C: Mika's mother said she had a new recipe that she wanted to try.

3. D: Mika said she wanted something NOW because she was hungry, and she wanted something to eat right away. She did not want to wait for the crackers to bake.

4. B: The items needed to make the crackers are listed under the word "ingredients." Therefore, "ingredients" means the items necessary to make a food or dish.

5. B: Butter is needed in step 2.

6. A: By saying to add the water "one tablespoon at a time," the writer is telling the cook to add the water a little bit at a time or gradually.

7. C: The writer listed the steps for making the cheese crackers in numerical order to show the importance of doing things in order when cooking.

8. A: Mika reads the cheese cracker recipe because she wants to make cheese crackers.

9. C: Now that she knows how to make cheese crackers, and she sees that they are easy to make, Mika probably will want to make them again with her mother.

10. D: Every spring, the class takes a trip to a historical museum.

11. A: Gerard, Hakeem's brother, warned him about the old war uniforms room where he heard strange noises and thought he saw a mannequin's eyes move.

12. D: That's just Sammy's imagination getting out of hand. This phrase tells the reader that Hakeem's mother thinks Sammy makes up things, and she does not trust his judgment.

13. C: Hakeem is not afraid of scary movies, and he laughed when he heard ghost stories by a campfire. This shows that Hakeem is brave and does not get scared easily.

14. B: Hakeem believes Gerard because his brother "does not joke around." Also, Hakeem did not think Gerard was trying to scare him, but rather was trying to warn him. This shows that Gerard is honest.

15. C: The flickering overhead light made the shadows around the mannequin's eyes jump. This made the eyes look like they were moving.

16. A: The small number of lamps and the one flickering bulb overhead gave the idea that the room was not lit well. Because of this, the word dim most likely means "badly lit."

17. D: Hakeem laughed because he found out that what his brother thought were ghosts actually were just creaking floorboards and a flickering bulb. He laughed because there was a logical explanation for the scary parts of the room.

18. B: Appearances can be deceiving. The creaking floorboards and jumping shadows mislead Gerard to think a ghost was in the room. What Gerard thought he saw turned out to be something completely different and safe.

19. C: Paragraph 2 says that, when Neil Armstrong was 14, his family moved back to Wapakoneta permanently. In the sentence before that, it says that the family moved 20 times. The word *permanently* shows that something changed about how often the family moved. The passage also does not say that the family moved again. This shows that *permanent* must mean "for good," since the Armstrong family stayed in Wapakoneta for good. The passage does not show that the Armstrong family needed to be in Wapakoneta by a certain day, so choice A is incorrect. The passage also does not say what time of day they moved, so choice B is incorrect. The passage does not mention other events that happened when the Armstrong family moved, so choice D is incorrect.

20. C: The section title "First Man on the Moon" shows that the section under that title is about Neil Armstrong being in the group of astronauts that walked on the moon. The year that Neil Armstrong walked on the moon is the most likely detail to be included in this section. The high school Neil Armstrong went to and the number of siblings he had would most likely be mentioned in the section titled "Armstrong's Childhood." This means choices A and D are incorrect. Choice B is not related to Neil Armstrong walking on the moon, so choice B is also incorrect.

21. D: This passage tells events in chronological order. It describes how Neil's childhood and early career led him to work for NASA and go to the moon. This means choice D is correct. The passage does not describe the history of NASA. It only mentions the year that NASA was created, so choice A is incorrect. The passage does not talk about Neil Armstrong's teachers or how he learned to fly a spaceship. Choices B and C are incorrect.

22. B: These titles use words and phrases like *childhood*, *career*, and *later life*. These words and phrases are related to parts of Neil Armstrong's life. The text under each section title describes the events that took place during a certain part of his life. Choice B is correct. Choice A is incorrect because only the section "Armstrong's Childhood" tells where he lived. Choice C is incorrect because the section "Armstrong's Childhood" does not talk about Neil Armstrong having a job. Choice D is incorrect because the passage only talks about one of Neil Armstrong's missions.

23. C: Paragraph 3 says that Neil Armstrong started college at Purdue University but stopped to join the military. It says that, later, he "came back to finish his college degree." This means that he finished his classes at college and was able to graduate from Purdue. In this sentence, *degree* is used to show that he finished college. This paragraph does not talk about heat or angles, so choices A and D are incorrect. Choice C is incorrect because *degree* is not being used to describe something in this sentence.

24. A: Paragraph 5 describes what Neil Armstrong did after he worked for NASA as an astronaut. It says he chose to become a professor instead of enjoying his fame. Choice A is correct, since this paragraph describes Neil Armstrong choosing a humble life. The paragraph does not say that Neil Armstrong was shy or that he did not know about politics, so choices B and C are incorrect. Choice D is incorrect because Neil Armstrong was a successful astronaut and is still remembered today.

25. B: The passage talks about Neil Armstrong's accomplishments and says that his life was "out of this world." This supports the conclusion that he will be remembered as a historical figure, so choice B is correct. The passage does not say that other astronauts must have a degree or pilot's license, so choice A is incorrect. It also does not mention any astronauts walking on the moon since

Neil Armstrong and his team, so choice C is incorrect. The passage does not talk about Neil Armstrong and President Kennedy meeting or becoming friends, so choice D is incorrect.

26. D: Sniffles, sneezing, coughing, and a red nose are all symptoms of a cold.

27. B: The mother tucks her into bed.

28. C: The medicine is purple and thick and tastes like grapes.

29. A: The author likes having her mother's full attention when she is sick.

30. D: Each paragraph in this passage focuses on telling the reader about Mercury, so choice D is correct. There are eight planets in the solar system, but only three are mentioned in the passage, so choice B is incorrect. The number of days in a year is part of a supporting detail in the passage. However, it is not the central idea, so choice B is incorrect. The Sun is mentioned multiple times in this passage. However, the passage is about Mercury, not the Sun, making choice C incorrect.

31. C: Paragraph 1 says that Mercury is barren and that there is nothing but soil on the surface. This includes plants. The author is trying to show the reader that there is no life on the planet. In this sentence, the word *barren* is used as a synonym for *lifeless,* making choice C correct. Paragraph 1 also says that Mercury has many craters. This means that Mercury is not smooth, so choice B is incorrect. The fact that Mercury's surface is covered in soil shows that its surface is not blue in color. This shows that *barren* does not mean *blue*, so choice A is incorrect. Mercury is a small planet, and there are no words in the passage that suggest that it is very big. This means that *barren* cannot mean *gigantic*, so choice D is incorrect.

32. B: The passage says that the name *Mercury* came from Ancient Rome and that Ancient Rome existed about 24 centuries ago. A century is 100 years, so Ancient Rome existed 2,400 years ago. However, Rome still exists today. This means that the phrase "Ancient Rome" is talking about things that happened in Rome a very long time ago, meaning choice B is the correct answer. The passage does not talk about how far away Rome is, so choice A is incorrect. Rome was and is a real place, so choice D is incorrect. *Recent* means something happened or existed not long ago. This has a meaning that is the opposite of the explanation given in the passage, so choice C is incorrect.

33. B: The introductory sentence of paragraph 4 says that humans will never live on Mercury. The concluding sentence also says this. The supporting details in paragraph 4 explain why people cannot live on Mercury's surface. This means that choice B is correct. The paragraph does not explain why there are extreme temperatures on Mercury, so choice C is incorrect. Paragraph 3 explains that a day on Mercury is as long as about 58 days on Earth. This means that choice A is incorrect. The passage does not talk about seasons on Mercury, so choice D is incorrect.

34. C: This diagram shows the reader what order the planets are in and how far each one is from the Sun. This means that the diagram shows the reader how close Mercury is to the Sun, so choice C is correct. This picture does not help the reader understand how Mercury was discovered, so choice A is incorrect. The temperatures on Mercury and the way it got its name are related to how close it is to the Sun. However, the diagram's main purpose is to help the reader see how close Mercury is to the Sun, so choices B and D are incorrect.

35. A, D: The two words that are synonyms of *inquisitive* are curious and interested. The sentence gives some context clues that helps to guide you to the synonyms. Peter always enjoyed going to the zoo, which implies that he was not afraid as in choice E. The sentence also uses the phrase "that he had never seen before," which is related to curiosity and interest. It can be concluded that Peter was curious and interested in seeing new animals. The zoo trip was real and did not have anything to do with imagination as in choice B. Nothing in the sentence refers to honesty (choice C).

36. D: Patricio Suarez is having the party.

37. B: The address for the party, 1234 Main Street, El Paso, is beside the word "where."

38. A: The day and time of the party, which is 2 p.m., is next to "when."

39. D: The invitation says that Patricio is having a birthday party.

40. C: Next to "bring," the invitation says "bathing suit." From this, one can infer that swimming will be the main activity at the party.

Online Resources

Due to our efforts to try to keep this book to a manageable length, we've created a link that will give you access to all of your online resources:

mometrix.com/resources719/vsolg3

It's Your Moment, Let's Celebrate It!

Share your story @mometrixtestpreparation